FACTS AT YOUR FINGERTIPS

ENDANGERED ANIMALS
FISH

BROWN
BEAR
BOOKS

OLDHAM COUNTY PUBLIC LIBRARY
308 YAGER AVENUE
LAGRANGE, KY 40031

Published by Brown Bear Books Limited

4877 N. Circulo Bujia
Tucson, AZ 85718
USA

and

First Floor
9-17 St. Albans Place
London N1 ONX
UK

Library of Congress Cataloging-in-Publication Data

Fish / edited by Tim Harris.
   p. cm. – (Facts at your fingertips. Endangered animals)
Includes bibliographical references and index.
 Summary: "Describes various fish that are endangered and at risk
of becoming extinct. Data Sheet sidebars and maps accompany
the text"–Provided by publisher.
 ISBN 978-1-936333-32-5 (library binding)
1. Rare fishes–Juvenile literature. 2. Endangered species–Juvenile
literature. I. Harris, Tim. II. Title. III. Series.

QL617.7.F57 2012
597.168–dc22

2010053976

ISBN-13 978-1-936333-32-5

Editorial Director: Lindsey Lowe
Editor: Tim Harris
Creative Director: Jeni Child
Designer: Lynne Lennon
Children's Publisher: Anne O'Daly
Production Director: Alastair Gourlay

Printed in the United States of America

In this book you will see the following key at top left of each entry. The key shows the level of threat faced by each animal, as judged by the International Union for the Conservation of Nature (IUCN).

EX	Extinct
EW	Extinct in the Wild
CR	Critically Endangered
EN	Endangered
VU	Vulnerable
NT	Near Threatened
LC	Least Concern
O	Other (this includes Data Deficient and Not Evaluated)

For a few animals that have not been evaluated since 2001, the old status of Lower Risk still applies and this is shown by the letters **LR** on the key.

For more information on Categories of Threat, see pp. 54–57.

Picture Credits

Abbreviations: c=center; t=top; l=left; r=right.

Cover Images
Front: *Lionfish*, Shutterstock/NIkita Tiunov
Back: *Whale shark*, Shutterstock/Brandelet

AL: Edwin Mickelburgh 61; **Aqualog:** 29 inset, 42–43; **Aquarian Fish Foods:** 49; **BCC:** Hans Reinhard 13; **FLPA:** Frants Hartmann 57, Linda Lewis 5b; **IUCN:** 59; **PEP:** Ken Lucas 37 inset; Peter Scoones 9; **Photolibrary Group:** Tony Bomford 22–23; Marty Cordano 56, Tui De Roy 58, Fredrick Ehrenstrom 39; Andreas Hartl/Okapia 14–15, Richard Hermann 4–5, 25, Stan Osolinski 54–55, Carl Roessler/Animals Animals 10–11, Norbert Rosing 58–59, Norbert Wu 47; **Photoshot:** A.N.T 45, G.I. Bernad 29, David Woodfall 7; **PX:** Max Gibbs 17t, 17b, 19, 20–21, 31, 37; **Joe Tomelleri:** 35; **U.S. Fish and Wildlife Service:** Richard Biggins; **Windmill Books:** Bown Bowen

Artwork © Brown Bear Books Ltd

Brown Bear Books has made every attempt to contact the copyright holder. If you have any information please email smortimer@brownbearbooks.co.uk

CONTENTS

What is a Fish?

Everyone can recognize a fish. At least, everyone thinks they can...until they begin to explore the term "fish" in a little detail.

Exceptions to the Rules

It is, of course, quite ridiculous to state that an animal is a fish just because it lives in water (dolphins, whales, leeches, lobsters, sea cucumbers, and numerous other aquatic organisms destroy this argument right away). It could be said that a fish can be identified by the fact that it has scales on its body, but that again is misleading. There are other organisms, such as reptiles (crocodiles, turtles, lizards, and so on) that have scales but are not fish. Even such animals as birds have scales (on their legs).

The other side of this coin is that not all animals that are known to be fish have scales. For example, catfish of the family Pimelodidae are naked. There are also numerous other examples of scaleless fish. All fish, however, have gills. But so have other aquatic

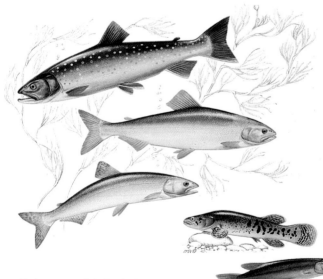

Salmon *and their relatives exhibit the classic characteristics we associate with fish, but these characteristics are not common to all fish.*

The oceanic sunfish is a giant of the open seas that does not fit the traditional image of what a fish should be like.

organisms. Newt larvae, salamander tadpoles, and the incredible neotenous axolotl (salamandrid) have gills, yet they are not fish.

We can make another rule: Fish are not only aquatic and have gills, they also have fins. This still fails as a definition, however, because there are animals such as cuttlefish and squids that are aquatic, breathe by means of gills, and have fins; yet these animals are mollusks. One important distinguishing factor, though, is that in cuttlefish and squids the internal organs are found inside a mantle cavity.

Fish do not have a mantle cavity. They do, however, have an internal skeleton, but so have cuttlefish and squids (the cuttlebone and pen, respectively). So do starfish and their close relatives, the urchins (their skeleton consists of calcareous plates overlain with thin surface tissue). What cuttlefish and urchins do not have is a cranium (braincase, or skull). Here, at last, is the definitive characteristic...or is it? Not quite. If it were, then lampreys and the other "jawless fish" would also be "real" fish—but they are not generally regarded as being so. They do have a skull of sorts, even though it is largely a covered cartilage "trough." However, they have so many other nonfish characteristics—the absence of a backbone, two (instead of three) semicircular canals in the ear, gills that are arranged almost back-to-front when compared with "normal"

- have a braincase and limb (fin) skeleton consisting of cartilage or bone
- have fins, usually—but not invariably—with spines or rays
- breathe through outwardly directed gills covered by an operculum (gill cover), which results in an external slitlike aperture or a series of gill slits
- have bodies covered in scales (there are some important exceptions here)
- have an air/swim-bladder used in buoyancy control (again, there are exceptions, as in sharks)
- have a sensory organ known as the lateral line organ running in a head/tail direction or another series of sensory pits (there are exceptions, as in sharks)
- are cold-blooded (poikilothermic)—so their body temperature matches that of the environment (there are some significant exceptions, such as tuna, which can raise their body temperature well above that of the surrounding water).

The History of Fish

It is generally accepted that life began in water some 3 billion years ago. For many millions of years after that, however, there does not appear to have been any major surge leading to the emergence of complex organisms. Indeed, it took about 2.4 billion years for the first animals that could be regarded as invertebrates to appear. From that point on the pace accelerated, to the extent that it took the relatively short time of about 120 million years for the first vertebrates to evolve. These aquatic creatures, known from fossils dating back about 480 million years, were the first fish. At least, we tend to refer to them as fish; but bearing in mind the numerous criteria, these creatures were very different from their modern-day equivalents. Nonetheless, they form the basal stock from which not just fish, but all other vertebrates evolved.

fish (in jawless fish they are directed internally)—that they cannot be regarded as "true" fish. In addition, jawless fish (Agnatha), as their name suggests, do not have jaws.

The almost inevitable conclusion of all this is that there really is no such thing as a fish!

A Common-Sense Approach

When we use the term fish, we should appreciate that it is a very broad-ranging word indeed, as broad, in fact, as the term "tetrapod," which means four-legged animal.

When the term "fish" is used, it generally refers to aquatic species that can be split into two groups:

- Cartilaginous fish (class Chondrichthyes): sharks, rays, chimeras (about 700 species).
- Bony fish (class Osteichthyes): all other species, from guppies to seahorses (well over 20,000 species).

It is possible, albeit with difficulty and numerous exceptions, to list the characteristics that, in combination, allow us to recognize a fish as such. Fish:

The seahorse, *with its forward-curled tail and horselike head, may not look like a fish–but it is.*

The earliest fish were jawless, a feature still retained by some of today's aquatic vertebrates like the hagfish and lampreys. Fish having true jaws (the acanthodians) did not evolve for another 40 to 50 million years, and it is from them that the present-day fish have arisen, with numerous extinctions along the way. Among these extinctions are the acanthodians themselves, which disappeared after about 150 million years. Another group—the antiarchs—had a shorter history, surviving for about 70 million years, having first emerged 400 million years ago.

The fossil record is incomplete, of course, so some of our interpretations have to be based on partial information. Nonetheless, the record is sufficiently wide ranging and representative for some major conclusions to be drawn. For instance, we can say that bichirs (family Polypteridae) have been around for 135 million years or so. Likewise, lungfish (families Ceratodontidae and Lepidosirenidae) have long histories stretching back to Devonian times (400 to 350 million years).

Most famous of all these so-called "living fossils" is the coelacanth (pp. 8–9), the first genuine remains of which occur in Devonian rocks and the last in 70-million-year-old sediments. After that time no more fossil coelacanths are found, so the line was assumed to have become

extinct. Then, in 1938 a living specimen was raised by fishermen off the Comoro Islands in the Indian Ocean. Others have followed over the years, leading to increased knowledge of this fascinating fish, which appears to have undergone no major changes when compared to the youngest of the known fossils.

Why are Fish at Risk?

Few places on our planet appear to be free of human influences, although sometimes they do not cause problems for the continued survival of a particular species. In fact, there are instances of both animals and plants that actually benefit from such situations. Sparrows and European blackbirds are just two of many species that might not be as numerous as they are today if they did not live in close proximity to humans and human-influenced environments. Broadly speaking, though, human influences often place species under greater pressure than they would normally experience.

Fish also have to cope with the consequences of habitat alteration, as other animals do. In the case of migratory species—like salmon, sturgeon (pp. 12–13), and others—dams, reservoirs, river channelization, and other changes can present insurmountable hurdles as the fish try to reach their spawning grounds upriver. In the worst cases local populations, or even species, can be driven to extinction as a result.

Hunters, *prey, and scavengers existed in prehistoric times, just as they do today. Here a large Glyptolepis (1) hunts a shoal of small Paleospondylis (2), while two Pterichthyodes (3) scavenge along the bottom.*

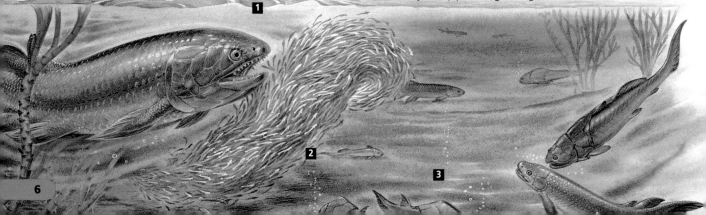

Rainbow trout *killed by an oil seepage into the water. Pollution of the waters poses serious threats to the survival of fish species around the world.*

In many other instances it is not changes in the quality of the water or the migratory routes that pose the greatest risks, but the restricted distribution of the species concerned. When this restriction is extreme (as is the case for the devil's hole pupfish, and bandula barb, pp. 30–31, for instance), the threat is so serious that stringent measures are required to ensure the survival of the species.

Ironically, one of the biggest threats that some fish have to face is posed by other fish. There are countless instances of fish being introduced into habitats outside their own natural range. It may be done to cater to a demand for sport or angling species (as in the case of trout) or as a means of providing a new source of animal protein for local communities (as in the case of the Nile perch introduction into Lake Victoria), or even to combat disease (as in the case of the mosquito fish, which has been widely introduced for biological control of malarial mosquitoes).

In many of these cases the introduced exotic species places the native species under threat. It could be through direct predation on adults or young or eggs, competition for space, competition for food or spawning sites, or, quite simply, through having a higher reproductive rate than the endemic species. There are several examples of fish that face such situations (such as mojarra caracolera, Lake Victoria cichlids, pp. 16–17, gold sawfin goodeid, and Lake Wanam rainbowfish).

Overfishing is also a major factor affecting abundance, with some species being placed under such survival pressures that only drastic action, including (but not restricted to) total or partial bans, can hope to save them from extinction. Species as diverse as tuna, cod, and shark all fall within this category, but there are many, many more.

The Situation Today

The IUCN 2000 Red List concluded that there was evidence of "an extremely serious deterioration, especially in the status of riverine species." An increase of 18 species on the Red List from 1996 to 2000 did not, at first sight, appear too drastic (see table). However, between 2000 and 2010 there was a dramatic increase in the number of endangered species, in part because of the problems faced by freshwater fish. More than 35 percent of North American freshwater species, for example, are now threatened. And the IUCN's forecast in 2000, that "It is highly probable that increased attention to these species by the Species Survival Commission over the next three years will confirm a worldwide global crisis in freshwater fish...." was confirmed.

Even allowing for the possibility that some of the increases may be the result of more accurate recording than in the past, we are still facing a grave situation; we need to do all that we can to reverse the trend.

Numbers of Threatened Species of Fish			
	1996	2000	2010
Critically Endangered	157	156	376
Endangered	134	144	400
Vulnerable	443	452	1,075
TOTAL	734	752	1,851

From 2000 to 2010 (see above) there was an increase of 1,099 threatened species of fish.

Coelacanth

Latimeria chalumnae

Until the late 1930s it was thought that the coelacanth had been extinct for 70 million years. Closely related to the ancestors of land vertebrates and so-called living fossils, the coelacanths alive today are primitive deep-sea bony fish. The name refers to the fish's hollow fin spines (the Greek koilos means "hollow" and akantha means "spine").

In 1938 a fishing boat was trawling at a depth of about 240 feet (70 m) off the coast of South Africa near Port Elizabeth when the crew spotted an unusual fish in the catch; none of them had ever seen one like it before. On returning to port, they informed Marjorie Courtenay-Latimer, curator of the local natural history museum. She could not identify it.

Marjorie Courtenay-Latimer measured, examined, and photographed the fish and then had it stuffed. She also wrote to James Leonard Brierly Smith, an ichthyologist (fish specialist) in Grahamstown in South Africa, enclosing a sketch.

The fish measured about 5 feet (1.5 m) in length and was mauvish-blue with iridescent silver markings. Its odd-looking fins were perhaps its most unusual feature. The caudal (tail) fin had an extra portion sticking out at the end, like an additional fin lobe. There were also two dorsal (back) fins, instead of one. The paired fins were even more strange in that they had "stems" that looked like limbs, with fin rays fanning out at the edges.

Fossil Record

The rest, as they say, is history. The fish was a coelacanth, a primitive marine bony fish of the genus *Latimeria*. Fish of the genus *Coelacanthus* had been found as fossils in rocks from the end of the Permian period—225 million years ago—and at the end of the Jurassic period 136 million years ago. The coelacanths were believed to have become extinct about 70 million years ago, so the find was a rare creature, a "living fossil." As such, it provoked much public interest. The modern coelacanth was larger than most fossil fish and had a powerful body.

Reports of other catches of coelacanths have been recorded in more recent years. However, none of the catches has occurred in South Africa until the latest finds in Sodurana Bay. Until the late 1990s the 200 or so finds all came from the waters around Comoros, a small group of islands between southeastern Africa and Madagascar in the Indian Ocean. However, in September 1997 Mark

DATA PANEL

Coelacanth

Latimeria chalumnae

Family: Latimeriidae

World population: Unknown

Distribution: Comoro Islands, Indian Ocean (between Madagascar and southeastern Africa); Sulawesi coelacanth (*Latimeria menadoensis*) lives only in oceans around Sulawesi, Indonesia

Habitat: Cold waters in deep ocean at 240 ft (70 m)

Size: Length: up to 5.9 ft (1.8 m). Weight: 210 lb (95 kg)

Form: Primitive fish with limblike pectoral fins. Bluish base color with light pinkish-white patches

Diet: Fish

Breeding: Livebearer (gives birth to living young). Up to 20 large eggs, each measuring 3.5 in (9 cm) in diameter and weighing 10.6–12.4 oz (300–350 g) are released from ovaries into oviduct. Developing embryos reach a length of at least 12 in (30 cm) before birth. Life span at least 11 years

Related endangered species: Sulawesi coelacanth VU

Status: IUCN CR

TANZANIA
COMOROS
MOZAMBIQUE
MADAGASCAR

Erdman, a scientist visiting the Indonesian island of Sulawesi, saw an unusual-looking fish being taken into the local market; he immediately identified it as a coelacanth. In 1998 a further specimen was found near Sulawesi, questioning the long-held belief that coelacanths inhabited a limited range in the Indian Ocean—Sulawesi is separated from the Comoro Islands by more than 6,000 miles (10,000 km). The Sulawesi coelacanths are similar apart from their coloration—they are brown with golden flecks. Analysis of genetic structures, however, indicated that the fish is a separate species with a population thought to be fewer than 10,000 mature adults.

Keeping the Past Alive

Although it is not possible to gauge exactly how many coelacanths there are, there is no doubt that they are very rare.

In recognition of its rarity CITES has listed the coelacanth under Appendix I, thus making trade in the fish illegal. Another protective measure involves the safe release of any specimens accidentally caught by fishermen. The coelacanth favors cold waters at depths of about 240 feet (70 m). A "deep release kit" (first suggested by Raymond Walner, a visitor to one of the coelacanth websites) allows specimens to be lowered rapidly in a sack to a depth where the water is sufficiently cold and where the fish can release itself safely. So far the method has proved to be the most effective way of returning coelacanths to the wild.

Coelacanths *found today have changed little from their ancestors, although they are larger than most "fossil fish." They have powerful bodies and limblike fins, which they use to move themselves around on the sea bottom when they are looking for prey.*

Great White Shark

Carcharodon carcharias

The great white shark is a hunter par excellence. It frequents a wide range of habitats, and within its domain its success is matched only by that other major predator, the orca, or killer whale.

The great white shark is magnificently designed. Torpedo-shaped and armed with multiple rows of replaceable saw-edged triangular teeth, it also has a battery of receptors that almost defy human comprehension. It can sense its prey from distances of over 1 mile (1.6 km); low-frequency sound waves can be picked up from this distance by the shark's ears, while low-frequency vibrations in the water are detected by its hypersensitive lateral line system (a system of sensory organs that detect even the slightest pressure changes and vibrations).

In addition to its long-distance senses the shark has an acute ability to detect weak electrical fields, such as those emitted by fish and other prey. The tiny pulses of electricity are picked up by the ends of ducts (ampullae of Lorenzini) located on the shark's snout. Such is the sensitivity of the ampullae that some sharks can locate prey such as flatfish even if it is buried in the sand.

Sharks can also sense blood—the unmistakable "signal" sent out by injured prey—at extremely weak dilutions. In experiments to find out more about the shark's capacity to detect weak solutions, lemon sharks were shown to sense tuna remnants or "juice" at an incredibly weak dilution of one part juice to 25 million parts of water.

The shark's ability to detect movement in dim light is aided by a membranous reflecting layer of cells located under the retina in the eye. It acts as a mirror, reflecting rays back through the retina, reactivating the light-sensitive cells in the process, and thus optimizing the eye's ability to detect movement in even minimal levels of illumination. This exceptional

DATA PANEL

Great white shark

Carcharodon carcharias

Family: Lamnidae

World population: About 10,000

Distribution: Worldwide, but predominantly in warm-temperate and subtropical waters; may also be found in warmer areas. Only infrequently encountered in cold northern regions

Habitat: Wide range of habitats from surf line to offshore (rarely in mid-ocean). Found between the surface and depths of 820 ft (250 m) or more

Size: Unconfirmed reports refer to specimens in excess of 23 ft (7 m). Confirmed data, however, indicates a maximum size of 18–20 ft (5.5–6 m)

Form: Torpedo-shaped fish with saw-edged triangular teeth. System of sensory organs for detecting prey; light-sensitive membrane below retina for tracking movement in dim light

Diet: Mainly bony fish but also cartilaginous fish (including other sharks); marine mammals, including cetaceans (whales and dolphins) and pinnipeds (seals and sea lions)

Breeding: Gives birth to 5–10 live young (probably more) after a gestation period that could last as long as 1 year

Related endangered species: Whale shark (*Rhincodon typus*) VU

Status: IUCN VU

sensory system, combined with the other attributes possessed by sharks, has ensured their survival for over 200 million years.

Pressure from Humans

Exploitation by humans has taken its toll over the years. Direct killing for the entertainment of professional anglers or to obtain shark products for the souvenir trade has caused significant decline. Passive killing, with great white sharks being caught in nets set out for other target species, has also exerted pressure on populations, as have shark nets installed to protect bathers along shark-threatened coastlines.

The combined effects of these and other threats have led to a significant decline in great white shark numbers. The actual extent of this decline and the total number of great whites that remain in the wild are difficult to quantify. There are several reasons for this, including the diversity of nomadic and homing habits exhibited by the species. Some specimens, for

The great white shark *is an aggressive sea predator with a finely tuned sensory system. However, hunting and accidental killings by humans have taken their toll on population numbers.*

instance, tend to frequent relatively localized "territories," while others are known to roam over large distances. Another complicating factor is that, worldwide, the species is relatively scarce.

As a result, although a figure of 10,000 has been cited as a global total, it can only be approximate. Concerned by the decline, several countries have implemented protection programs. Measures range from banning all great white shark products to prohibiting activities such as fishing or underwater viewing by tourists. Further action is being urged by conservation bodies who fear that the current IUCN listing as Vulnerable may be incorrect and that the great white shark may already be Endangered.

Common Sturgeon

Acipenser sturio

It is difficult to imagine that some European rivers can hide giant fish measuring up to 20 feet (6 m) long that are capable of producing many millions of eggs in a single spawning. Such a fish is the common sturgeon. In spite of its prolific breeding habits, the species is at risk.

The common sturgeon usually grows to a length of 3.3 to 6.6 feet (1 to 2 m), but can be longer. At least one report indicates that the species can attain a length of 20 feet (6 m) and a weight of about 1,300 pounds (600 kg). Despite this report, probably the largest specimen actually on record was 11.3 feet (3.4 m) long and 705 pounds (320 kg). The female has the potential to deliver close to 2.5 million eggs in a single spawning episode.

As with some 40 or so other sturgeon species, the common sturgeon is under severe threat. It was once found in large numbers along the coast of Europe, from the North Sea to the Mediterranean and Black Seas. Today it is known only from the Garonne River and estuary, in France.

Sturgeons are famous primarily for their eggs, known universally as caviar. However, many species have also been fished for their flesh. All species are long-lived, with ages beyond 50 years being common.

Double Life

The common sturgeon is anadromous, which means that it spends its life at sea but migrates into freshwater habitats during the spawning season. One notable exception to the rule is the common sturgeon population that lives in Lake Ladoga in Russia. Another is the sterlet, which lives permanently in fresh water.

Spawning migrations upriver occur in early or mid-spring, with actual breeding taking place during early summer. Spawning is usually in pools that are several feet deep and have a flow of water. Alternatively, it may occur along river banks covered by spring floods. The eggs—up to 2.5 million for a largish female—are scattered over a gravelly bottom and abandoned.

By now the condition of the adults has deteriorated, since they do not feed during their migrations: Many, in fact, will not make it back to sea to resume feeding. In better days such losses would not have been a problem, owing to the large number of adults in the population, not to mention the high numbers of offspring. Today every adult that dies adds to the rarity of the species.

DATA PANEL

Common sturgeon (Baltic sturgeon)

Acipenser sturio

Family: Acipenseridae

World population: 20–750 mature individuals

Distribution: Garonne River and estuary, France

Habitat: Relatively shallow, mainly coastal seas, usually over sandy or muddy bottoms; some specimens move to deeper waters

Size: Length: on average 3.3–6.6 ft (1–2 m). Weight: a 10-ft (3-m) specimen may weigh about 440 lb (200 kg)

Form: Elongated body with distinct snout and characteristic caudal (tail) fin in which upper lobe is larger than lower one. Five rows of large, stout scales down body. Underslung mouth has distinctive barbels (whiskers)

Diet: Adults feed on bottom-dwelling marine invertebrates, but will also take small fish; juveniles feed mostly on bottom-dwelling freshwater invertebrates

Breeding: Migrates up to 620 miles (1,000 km) upriver in early to mid-spring; spawning occurs over gravel or pebbles, usually in flowing water pools. Each female is usually accompanied by more than 1 male. Hatching takes about 7 days, and juveniles may stay in their river of birth for up to 4 years

Related endangered species: In 2010 the IUCN listed 12 species of sturgeon as critically endangered; these include the ship sturgeon (*Acipenser nudiventris*) CR

Status: IUCN CR

Young common sturgeon stay fairly close to the spawning grounds at first, but gradually move downriver as they grow. Some reports suggest that by the fall of the same year they move out to sea; others state that this may be delayed for one to four years. Whatever the case, males mature at between seven and nine years (some estimates indicate later maturation between nine and 13 years), while females may take eight to 14 years (some estimate it to be between 11 and 18 years) to mature and return to their waters of birth to breed for the first time.

Overfishing and Habitat Destruction

Overfishing is usually cited as the main reason for the sharp decline in numbers. Undoubtedly, fishing has had a severe effect on natural populations, not just of the common sturgeon, but of many of its relatives. Some of the eastern populations and species in particular are still the focus of illegal trade in caviar. In some cases arguments have been put forward to ban fishing altogether. However, others argue that to do so would drive the market underground and into the hands of organized illegal groups, thus probably accentuating rather than solving the problem.

The common sturgeon's best hope for the future appears to lie in coordinated captive-breeding programs to rear stocks for commercial exploitation of the roe (caviar). Such farms are likely to produce more fish than may eventually be needed for harvesting purposes, thus acting as a potential source of fish for restocking former habitats. A beneficial spinoff from such programs is that they also reduce pressure on existing wild stocks.

However successful such breeding projects may be, the survival of the species in the wild needs to be urgently addressed. One problem is the pollution of watercourses. While it presents a daunting challenge, there are other potentially more difficult pressures facing the common sturgeon, including the building of dams, water channeling, and allied habitat-altering developments that plague the waterways.

The common sturgeon *has a number of distinctive features, including an elongated snout and barbels (whiskers) below its underslung mouth.*

Danube Salmon

Hucho hucho

Unlike its oceangoing cousins, the Danube salmon lives, breeds, and dies in the inland waters of the Danube River, where it is exposed to habitat destruction and environmental pollution.

Salmon are majestic fish, and the Danube species is the largest of all. While the Danube salmon lives in rivers, many species live at sea. On reaching maturity, sea-dwelling salmon undertake a migration of epic proportions to the river in which they were spawned. Compelled by instinct, each fish battles against unbelievable odds—sometimes including rapids or even falls—to reach the mouth of its home river to spawn. The female digs pits in the gravel in which to lay her eggs, which take about five weeks to hatch.

Although the life cycle of sea-dwelling salmon is physically challenging, its migratory habits have helped safeguard its success as a species. Juveniles that manage to negotiate the journey from their spawning grounds to the sea stand a better chance of reaching maturity than those that stay in the rivers of their birth. Unlike the Danube salmon, sea salmon avoid exposure to the pollution or irreversible habitat alteration that can occur in rivers as a result of environmental disasters.

International Pressures

The Danube River flows through 12 countries inhabited by a total of more than 70 million people. Enforcement of environmental controls is therefore complicated. Some problems are historical, relating to industrial sites that were built before environmental

DATA PANEL

**Danube salmon
(European salmon,
Danube trout, European river trout)**

Hucho hucho

Family: Salmonidae

World population: Unknown; estimates are low

Distribution: Rivers of Danube basin; introduced elsewhere in Europe, U.S., Canada, and Morocco

Habitat: Deep, well-oxygenated regions of fast-flowing water; also found in backwaters at temperatures of 43–64°F (6–18°C)

Size: Up to 6.5 ft (2 m). Weight: over 220 lb (100 kg)

Form: Similar to salmon (*Salmo salar*), but slimmer; large head and jaws. Greenish back, silvery sides with diffused pink sheen, white along belly. Numerous small star-shaped black spots on back, gradually decreasing in number down body

Diet: Adults feed on other fish, amphibians, reptiles, waterfowl, and even small mammals. Juveniles feed predominantly on invertebrates

Breeding: Spawning March–May after migration to shallow, gravelly areas with fast-flowing, oxygen-rich water. Female excavates nest with tail and (with help of male) covers fertilized eggs. Hatching period 5 weeks

Related endangered species: Satsukimasa salmon (*Oncorhynchus ishikawai*) EN; carpione del Garda (*Salmo carpio*) CR; Ohrid trout (*S. letnica*) DD; ala Balik (*S. platycephalus*) CR; Adriatic salmon (*Salmothymus obtusirostris*) EN; beloribitsa (*Stenodus leucichthys leucichthys*) EW

Status: IUCN EN

The Danube salmon *(also known as the European salmon, Danube trout, and European river trout) is the largest of all the salmons, and faces an uncertain future.*

legislation had to be taken into account. Others are political, where one country is not bound by the environmental laws of another. Both situations apply to the Danube, along which there are approximately 1,700 industries, many producing wastes that are known to be toxic. Aquatic organisms cannot survive the levels of toxicity and must find new areas or perish. Escape is not always possible, and the result is often the destruction of many thousands of creatures and their habitats.

Pollution Crises

In 2000 a dam leaked cyanide from a Romanian gold mine into the Tiza River, a tributary of the Danube, killing all forms of aquatic life for 250 miles (400 km) downstream. In Hungary alone about 85 tons of dead fish were removed. Some environmentalists claimed that the whole ecological system of the river had been wiped out by the spillage.

By early February 2000 cyanide was detected at the confluence of the Tiza with the Danube, and it was feared that the poisoning might cause the extinction of the Danube salmon. The outcome has been less devastating, but the situation illustrates the precarious future faced by the Danube salmon.

Such pollution crises are serious enough to threaten the existence of any Danube species. In the case of the Danube salmon there are other significant threats, including overfishing, water extraction for a wide range of industrial and other uses, and river alteration (primarily channeling and damming).

The Danube salmon is being pressurized from many quarters, to the extent that its long-term survival looks uncertain. Repeated attempts to introduce hatchery-bred stocks into a number of watercourses have been largely unsuccessful. However, in 1968 stocks were introduced from Czechoslovakia into Spanish waters, well outside the species' natural range. Over the years the stocks have become established. Restocking might not be the answer to the Danube salmon's problems, but it could be an essential lifeline.

Lake Victoria Haplochromine Cichlids

Haplochromis spp.

Restricted by nature to a certain habitat, many animal and plant species will evolve into several types, to fill every possible niche with little or no overlap. Such "species flocks" are able to survive side by side without much competition. This is the situation in the Great Rift lakes of Africa.

Africa's three major lakes, or "inland seas"—Lakes Malawi, Tanganyika, and Victoria—contain a bewildering array of fish species so diverse and colorful that they are often compared with coral reef fish. Each lake has its own endemic species (species found nowhere else). Lake Malawi is famous for *Aulonocara*, *Melanochromis*, and *Pseudotropheus* species, while Lake Tanganyika has *Lamprologus*, *Neolamprologus*, and *Julidochromis* species. Lake Victoria is renowned for haplochromine cichlids.

DATA PANEL

Lake Victoria haplochromine cichlids

Haplochromis spp.

Family: Cichlidae

World population: Some 200 species are known to have become extinct since mid-1950s; population levels of remaining species are estimated to have decreased from about 80% of total biomass of the lake to about 1%

Distribution: Lake Victoria, East Africa

Habitat: Wide range of habitats mostly close to the lake bottom and in relatively shallow water

Size: Length: about 4 in (10 cm)

Form: Most species have laterally compressed bodies, large eyes and mouths, and well-formed fins. Dorsal (back) fin has spinous front half and soft-rayed back half. Males of most species exhibit egglike spots (egg dummies) on anal (belly) fin

Diet: Diverse, but specific to each species. Phytoplankton and zooplankton encrusting algae, insects, mollusks, crustaceans, eggs, larvae, or even scales of other fish

Breeding: Female lays small number of eggs (sometimes only 5, depending on size and species). Males stimulated to release sperm by females pecking at egg dummies. Eggs and sperm brooded orally by females; female guards young, taking them back into mouth if danger threatens

Related endangered species: All species of haplochromine in Lake Victoria

Status: Those listed by IUCN as CR include *Haplochromis sp. nov. '75', H. sp. nov. 'Amboseli,'* and *H. sp. nov. 'citrus'*

Lake Victoria

Lake Victoria is a massive body of fresh water. In surface dimensions it is the third largest lake in the world after Lake Superior and the Caspian Sea. It is, however, relatively shallow; its maximum depth is only 260 feet (80 m). Owing to its highly irregular coast profile, its shoreline is about 2,200 miles (3,500 km) long. Despite its colossal size, it is surrounded by land and is virtually cut off from major external influences. As a result, it has developed its own special characteristics, including hard and alkaline water.

Victoria Cichlids

Within this special environment habitats vary across the thousands of bays and inlets along the lake coastline, where a large number of fish species can be found. Estimates vary, but over 200—and probably closer to 400—endemic species of cichlids have evolved. More than half belong to the genus *Haplochromis*. Owing to the relative "youth" of Lake Victoria, the evolution of so many different cichlid species in such a short time has been referred to as an example of "explosive radiation," or "evolutionary avalanche."

Catastrophic Developments

A series of developments has affected these haplochromine populations. For example, pressures were created by a fast-expanding human population around the lake, and greater demand for arable land has resulted in forested areas

The emerald-backed cichlid (above) may be prey to the voracious Nile perch (below right) that was introduced to Lake Victoria in the 1950s.

being cleared. This has led to increased runoff into the lake—both physical (silt) and chemical (fertilizers)—and to changes in the vegetation of near-shore areas.

In addition, an increasing demand for protein arose. Traditionally gotten from fishing practiced at a sustainable level, the situation became critical when populations of some of the best food fish species dramatically collapsed. By the 1950s at least one species was commercially extinct. In order to provide people with a regular supply of cheap animal protein, two food fish species were introduced into the lake: Tilapia and the Nile perch.

For nearly 30 years there appeared to be no major change in the lake's endemic fauna. However, in 1980 a survey revealed a sudden drop in haplochromine cichlids. From originally forming about 80 percent by weight of catches, they had dropped to 1 percent, with 80 percent represented by the Nile perch.

The Nile perch fishing industry has become hugely important to the local economy. However, a large Nile perch consumes vast quantities of smaller fish. They are therefore blamed for the large-scale decimation leading to the extinction of about 50 percent of the lake's haplochromines. As a result, the Nile perch has turned to other foods, including its own young.

Ray of Hope

For the cichlids the future is still uncertain. Several national and international projects are, however, addressing factors concerning their continued survival. One such development is a wide-ranging captive-breeding program. Some 40 species have already been bred; and while rates of success vary, this is encouraging news. Additionally, aquaculture is being encouraged among the fishermen of the lake in the hope of reducing pressure on remaining cichlid stocks.

The Lake Victoria situation is complex. Yet with appropriate encouragement and dedication further losses may be prevented in the years to come.

Dragon Fish

Scleropages formosus

A fishing eagle hunting over the forests of central Sumatra spotted a large fish in the foaming waters of a stream below. It swooped from the skies, dived into the water, and mated with the armor-plated fish. Thus the dragon fish was born.

So went the legend of the dragon fish. As is often the case, the story is a somewhat fanciful explanation of the facts. The remarkable union between a fish and a bird seemed plausible given the large yolks to which baby dragon fish are attached during the first weeks of their development when they incubate inside their father's mouth. Dragon fish eggs have a spherical yolk that can measure up to 0.7 inches (1.8 cm) in diameter, making them larger than those of many bird species.

It is likely that the legend of the dragon fish was also reinforced by observations. People may have seen predatory birds attempting to prey on dragon fish, although the fish's thick, immensely strong scales probably protected it from such aerial attacks. If a fishing eagle or other bird of prey were to dive onto a dragon fish, causing a great deal of splashing and foaming in the process, the chances are that it would leave empty-handed (or empty-taloned). It is easy to see how a failed attack (or more likely many failed attacks observed over time) could have been interpreted as mating rather than hunting.

A Fish of Many Forms

Dragon fish are found in eastern Asia, including Malaysia, the Philippines, Vietnam, and Indonesia. Doubt exists about the Myanmar (Burma) populations, and the species may now be extinct in Thailand. The fish are known variously as the Asian arowana, Asian bonytongue, Malayan bonytongue, and emperor fish. In their native waters three names are regularly used: cherek kelesa, ikan arowana (in Malaysia), and Lóng Yú (in Chinese-speaking countries).

The dragon fish occurs in three color forms in the wild (with regional modifications):

DATA PANEL

Dragon fish

Scleropages formosus

Family: Osteoglossidae

World population: Unknown

Distribution: Cambodia, Malaysia, Philippines, Vietnam, Indonesia (Kalimantan and Sumatra). Possibly Myanmar (Burma); may now be extinct in Thailand

Habitat: Still or slow-flowing waters that may be turbid (muddy) or heavily vegetated

Size: Length: up to 35 in (90 cm); usually much smaller

Form: Torpedo-shaped body with pointed head, large eyes, and large mouth with barbels (whiskers). Thick, strong scales. Three color forms: green/silver, gold, and red

Diet: A wide range of invertebrates and small vertebrates may be eaten. They are usually taken from the surface or upper part of the water column, but may occasionally also be plucked off branches above water

Breeding: About 30 eggs (but as many as 90 or more) are laid and are incubated orally by the male for 5–6 weeks; main breeding season July–December. Mature at 3–4 years

Related endangered species: Spotted or southern saratoga *(Scleropages leichardti)* LRnt; pirarucu *(Arapaima gigas)* DD

Status: IUCN EN

The dragon fish, *particularly the red color form, is highly regarded throughout east Asia, where captive-breeding programs have ensured its survival.*

green/silver, gold, and red. The last of these is deemed the most valuable. Captive-bred varieties include crosses between the different color forms as well as color-selected types, such as the rainbow dragon. Occasionally, albinos have been reported.

Breeding can occur throughout the year, but is at its peak between July and December. Actual mating is preceded by a long period of courtship and bonding that can last two or three months. The females (which have a single ovary) will lay about 30 eggs—although over 90 have been reported—which, once fertilized, are picked up by the male in its mouth. From that point onward the female plays no further part in the process. The male, however, will incubate the eggs in its mouth for between five and six weeks, by which time the young fish (fry) can attain a length of nearly 3.5 inches (9 cm).

Fears for the Fish of Good Fortune

The dragon fish is held in high esteem in Asia, where it is believed to bring health, wealth, and luck to its owners. It is kept in aquaria throughout the region and is also much sought after by east Asian communities all over the world. Specialized Western aquarists are also interested in the species, but the large size that adult specimens can attain places the dragon fish outside the reach of most enthusiasts.

Fears for the continued survival of the dragon fish in the wild—probably as a result of overcollection—led to the species being listed under Appendix I of CITES in 1975. At one time the dragon fish was classified as Insufficiently Known by the IUCN, but its status has since been changed to Endangered.

Whether the concern over the fish's survival is fully justified or not remains open to debate. Populations have become established from captive-bred specimens in a government plan in Singapore. Monitored captive-breeding programs in other forms and other east Asian countries have also resulted in the establishment of registered farms that are licensed to export the species under a CITES Appendix I provision.

Silver Shark

Balantiocheilos melanopterus

Despite its name and a passing visual similarity to true sharks, the silver shark could not really be more different from its namesakes. It is not ferocious, it lacks true teeth, and it feeds on tiny insects and plants, rather than fish, squid, and other marine animals.

The silver shark is a popular aquarium fish. Ever since it was first imported into Europe in 1955, it has been in great demand worldwide, in particular the very attractively colored juveniles.

Shark Appeal

The label "shark" made the fish appealing to millions of aquarium keepers around the world, even though the freshwater aquarium fish are not related to their predatory, marine namesakes. Although there are many other, smaller, more colorful aquarium species, the demand for silver sharks is high.

The silver shark is a cyprinid (a member of the family Cyprinidae). The family includes other "sharks"—the red-tailed black shark, the rainbow or ruby shark, and the black shark; all have a profile with only superficial resemblance to a true shark.

One of the reasons for the popularity of the silver shark and other freshwater aquarium "sharks" is the relative ease with which they can be kept. They do not have exacting dietary or water chemistry demands, and assuming that appropriately roomy accommodation can be provided, it is perfectly possible to keep such fish in peak condition until they die of old age (after several years). Modern aquarium technology and husbandry techniques mean that even fully mature specimens of silver shark, or even the larger black shark, can be kept.

Wild Populations Under Pressure

At one time the silver shark was so abundant throughout its range in Southeast Asia that it was regarded as a Category I species for home aquaria.

DATA PANEL

Silver shark (bala shark, tricolor shark)

Balantiocheilos melanopterus

Family: Cyprinidae

World population: Virtually extinct in some parts of the range but more common in others

Distribution: Kalimantan (Borneo), Sumatra (Indonesia), Thailand, and peninsular Malaysia

Habitat: Flowing, oxygen-rich waters

Size: Up to 14 in (35 cm)

Form: Elongated fish with a passing resemblance to true sharks. Body almost entirely covered in silvery, highly reflective, scales. Pectoral (chest) fins uncolored, but others are golden yellow and black

Diet: Wide range of aquatic insects and other invertebrates; delicate submerged vegetation

Breeding: In the wild mass spawnings occur following migration to breeding grounds. Eggs are scattered among vegetation or over the substratum and abandoned by the spawners

Related endangered species: None

Status: IUCN EN

The term applies to species that are in demand and are collected or bred in large quantities for aquarists.

The fish stocks appeared to be inexhaustible; but, as in so many instances, they eventually proved not to be. Demand continued, and local populations became overfished, so the search expanded into unexploited areas, including spawning grounds. Harvests removed not only juveniles from a population, but also a percentage of the breeding adults that would normally replenish the numbers. Existing stocks were therefore placed under unsustainable pressure.

Further pressures came from deforestation, with the accompanying habitat alteration, deterioration in water quality, and siltation. Eventually, the silver shark became scarce in parts of its range within Kalimantan and Sumatra, and was virtually wiped out in others. Thailand populations, however, remained almost untouched, so the species as a whole was not depleted to a point beyond recovery. Today, however, the Thai populations are also believed to be declining.

In recent years the main cause of decline has not been collection from the wild; demand by aquarists for the silver shark is now met from captive-bred stocks. Wild populations still face an uncertain future, however, as a result of various factors, including habitat alteration, water deterioration caused by the use of chemicals, and the small-mesh nets used in fishing. The problems are being addressed, but it will be some time before the solutions can be assessed.

Silver sharks are members of the Cyprinidae family, which includes the food fish carp, roach, and tench; they are typically toothless fish with rounded, smooth-edged scales. The silver shark's scales are shiny and highly reflective.

Whale Shark

Rhincodon typus

The whale shark is the largest living fish in the world. However, unlike some other shark species, it is harmless to humans, feeding mainly on plankton. Ironically, its approachability has contributed to its decline; it has always been easy prey for fishermen.

Mature specimens of the whale shark are about 39 feet (just over 12 m), but can reach a length of 59 feet (18 m). The whale shark's closest rival in terms of size is the basking shark, which is about 33 feet (10 m) but can reach a length of 50 feet (nearly 15 m).

While they are undoubtedly sharks in every aspect of their biology, neither the whale shark nor the basking shark fits the description of a vicious predator, an image that is commonly associated with many sharks. Furthermore, unlike other shark species such as the tiger shark, blue shark, hammerhead shark, and the great white shark, the basking shark and whale shark have not been known to attack humans.

Whale sharks are sluggish animals and tend to swim close to the surface of the water. Like basking sharks, they feed on plankton, which they filter from the sea using gill rakers. (All other sharks feed on a variety of animals, including fish, squid, octopus, and other small sharks.)

Easy Prey

The whale shark's habit of forming large groups in certain areas of the world ensures that considerable numbers are seen by humans (including tourists, conservationists, and scientists). It may be that the whale shark's approachability—which makes it attractive to divers—has also played a significant role in raising people's awareness about its vulnerability and threatened survival. However, whale sharks have human predators, and local hunting has taken a severe toll on whale shark populations. For example, it is reported that as many as 1,000 whale

DATA PANEL

Whale shark

Rhincodon typus

Family: Rhincodontidae

World population: Unknown

Distribution: Atlantic, Indian, and Pacific Oceans

Habitat: Tropical and temperate waters, both inshore and deep sea

Size: Length: 39 ft (12 m); may grow to 59 ft (18 m)

Form: Whalelike shark with broad, flat head, truncated snout, and large mouth with small teeth. Grayish color, with patterns of light spots and stripes unique to each individual

Diet: Zooplankton, small fish, and other small animals

Breeding: Internal fertilization; female retains fertilized eggs, which hatch within her body; young measure 16–20 in (40–50 cm) at birth

Related endangered species: Basking shark (*Cetorhinus maximus*) VU; great white shark (*Carcharodon carcharias*) VU; porbeagle (*Lamna nasus*) VU; blacktip shark (*Carcharhinus limbatus*) NT; sandbar shark (*C. plumbeus*) VU; Ganges shark (*Glyphis gangeticus*) CR; bluntnose six-gill shark (*Hexanchus griseus*) LRnt; sand tiger shark (*Carcharias taurus*) VU; dusky shark (*C. obscurus*) VU; kitefin shark (*Dalatias licha*) NT

Status: IUCN VU

sharks were killed by fishermen from just three Indian villages in one year. Statistics such as these immediately raise the question: Can the world population of whale sharks sustain such a level of hunting? No one knows whether there are separate populations of whale sharks or just one single, migratory world population. If there is only one population, then sustained removal at the level of 1,000 or more creatures a year will be extremely harmful to the species.

Limited Knowledge

Information about whale sharks is extremely limited. For example, no one knows how many whale sharks exist worldwide or details of their growth rate and life span. There are numerous other aspects of their biology that are not yet understood. Ironically, a lack of knowledge is one of the reasons that the whale

Despite their great size, *whale sharks are placid creatures, and divers can approach them safely. They are slow moving and tend to swim close to the surface of the water.*

shark has not been regarded as a commercially exploitable species.

Action is now being taken by several countries to gather information about the whale shark; at the same time, measures are being implemented to protect existing populations. Conservation programs have also been set up on the eastern seaboard of the United States, as well as in the Maldives, the Philippines, and Western Australia. It is hoped that data from the various projects can be used to help ensure the whale shark's survival. The expansion of such measures to include other regions used by whale sharks is another step in the right direction.

EX
EW
CR
EN
VU
NT
LC
O

Northern Bluefin Tuna

Thunnus thynnus

Tuna are the long-distance specialists of the fish world, covering several thousand miles a year on their migrations. They are also among the fastest-swimming fish in the world. Some populations are now endangered as a result of the world demand for tuna meat.

Tuna are fish built for speed. Every aspect of their body form is suited to maximum performance in the water. Their body is fusiform (pointed at both ends) with a stiff, sickle-shaped caudal (tail) fin perfect for producing maximum thrust. The bluefin tuna also has several features designed to reduce water resistance. Its scales are tiny and lie tightly against the skin, so minimizing friction. Its large eyes are well-bedded within their sockets, so the outer layer lies flush with the skin surface. The two dorsal (back) fins and the single anal (belly) fin fit into grooves when they are folded, while the series of finlets between the fins and the tail allow water to flow between them. The pectoral (chest) and pelvic (hip) fins are small and have a stiff front edge, which prevents them from collapsing when they are extended at high speeds.

A striking feature of the tuna's body is the deep-red color of the muscle tissue. This characteristic is found in the family Scombridaea that includes other high-speed species such as mackerel, bonitos, and their relatives. Red muscle has a rich blood supply that is typical of a species constantly on the move. The blood supplies the high levels of oxygen that the fish need and gives them plenty of stamina.

However, tuna would be unable to maintain their constant day-and-night swimming at speed were it not for a further adaptation. Unlike the majority of fish whose internal body temperature matches that of their environment, a tuna's countercurrent blood circulation allows it to maintain a high internal body temperature whatever the water temperature.

All-Consuming Demand

Bluefin tuna have been fished for about 100 years. Originally only sport fishermen and a few small-scale

DATA PANEL

Northern bluefin tuna (Atlantic bluefin tuna)

Thunnus thynnus

Family: Scombridae

World population: Disputed: about 40,000 in the western Atlantic (no equivalent data available for the eastern Atlantic)

Distribution: Atlantic. On eastern side from Norway to Mediterranean Sea, along western African coast to Cape Blanc. On western side from Newfoundland south to Brazil. Seen in central and northwestern Pacific

Habitat: Open oceanic waters

Size: Length: 15 ft (4.6 m). Weight: up to 1,320 lb (600 kg)

Form: Fusiform (spindle-shaped), streamlined body. Coloration deep blue above, with purple or green iridescence (colors that shimmer as observer changes position); silvery sides and belly

Diet: Fish (including herring, mackerel, and whiting); also squid

Breeding: Spawning occurs in the Gulf of Mexico, the western Atlantic, and in the

Mediterranean Sea in the east. Western stocks spawn from mid-April to mid-June; their eastern counterparts breed from June–August. Female can release about 30 million eggs

Related endangered species: Albacore tuna (*Thunnus alalunga*) DD; bigeye tuna (*T. obesus*) VU; southern bluefin tuna (*T. maccoyii*) CR; Monterrey Spanish mackerel (*Scomberomorus concolor*) EN

Status: IUCN DD (western population CR; eastern population EN)

enterprises supplying fish for human consumption fished the species. But starting in the 1930s—and continuing for the next 30 to 40 years—sport fishing soared in popularity.

Then in the 1970s a new commercial dimension was added to the sports angling industry, arising out of the fast-expanding demand for fresh (deep-frozen) tuna meat in Japan. The market for raw tuna provided by sushi and sashimi enthusiasts led to 40 percent of the global tuna catch being sent to the Japanese market. A major factor leading to the rapid expansion was the improvement in air freight and transport that began in the 1970s and made possible transglobal overnight deliveries of fresh-caught tuna.

Allied to major changes that had occurred within the commercial fishery—which had also led to ever-greater catches—the fishing of large tuna by sport anglers for profit as well as sport led to dramatically declining yields in the space of a few years. Total Atlantic harvests of bluefin tuna plummeted from a peak of 38,600 tons (35,000 tonnes) in 1964 to less than half—18,500 tons (16,800 tonnes)—by 1972. By the early 1980s catches in the western Atlantic had dropped even further to about 6,600 tons (6,000 tonnes). A report by the International Commission for

Northern bluefin tuna *are superbly adapted to their environment in shape and structure. The deep blue color on the back and pale-colored belly also makes them hard for predators to see from above or below.*

the Conservation of Atlantic Tunas (ICCAT) has estimated that by the early 1990s the population of adult bluefins in the western Atlantic had dropped to just 13 percent of its 1975 level.

Population Conundrum

Fishing controls have been introduced to protect the northern bluefin tuna, and these are regularly reviewed. In 2011, for example, it was agreed that the quota of fish caught in the eastern Atlantic be reduced by 4 percent to 14,220 tons (12,900 tonnes), although some scientists argued that this figure was still too large. The situation is complicated because there is no consensus on population levels.

Meanwhile, tagging programs, aerial surveys, captive breeding, and genetic analysis are some of the methods being used to establish the status of the bluefin tuna on both sides of the Atlantic. This should pave the way for enforcing realistic fishing controls.

Masked Angelfish

Genicanthus personatus

The rare and exceptionally beautiful masked angelfish is found on the Hawaiian Islands. The males are so differently colored from the females that they could pass as a separate species, and intriguingly, the females are able to change sex. No one knows quite how rare the fish is, but it has never been observed in large numbers.

In the early 1970s four specimens of a previously unknown dwarf angelfish were collected by aquarium divers off Hawaii and Oahu. All four specimens were females. They had an ivory-white body with mainly white fins. The tail fin was half white and half black, and the head carried a black "mask." The species was named masked angelfish.

At the time of their description John Randall, an ichthyologist (zoologist specializing in fish), predicted that when males were eventually found, they would turn out to be quite different from the females. Two years later, in 1975, he was proved right when two males were collected in a trawl by a research vessel. The mature specimens retained the white body (tinted with some gray) and black tail band of the female. However, the mask was not black, but an intense yellow-gold; so were all the other fins. In fact, the males were so differently colored that they could easily have been described as a new species of *Genicanthus*.

Angels and Butterflies

Up until the mid-1970s angelfish were grouped with butterflyfish in a single family, but there are several characteristics that separate the two groups. In particular, angelfish have a stout, backward-pointing spine on the preopercle (the bone that lies directly in front of the operculum or gill cover proper). It is absent in butterflyfish, which have either a smooth-edged preopercle or one with serrated edges. The lack of a spine, added to other skeletal differences, was eventually deemed significant enough to raise the status of each group and to give them families of their own: the family Pomacanthidae for angelfish and the family Chaetodontidae for butterflyfish.

For a long time little was known about the reproductive biology of angelfish. In 1978, however, a study carried out on the Japanese pygmy angel revealed a most interesting characteristic: the fish could change sex, but only in one direction. The Japanese pygmy angel is usually found in groups or harems consisting of a single, dominant male and several females. However, if the male is removed by a predator, for example, the top-ranking female (usually the largest) gradually changes sex over a period of two to three weeks and becomes a fully functional male. Following similar reports for other angelfish species, it soon became evident that sex change (from female to male, but not in the other direction) was fairly widespread. As yet, it is not known if every species of angelfish has this ability, but the masked angelfish certainly does.

Captive Angels

In the past nearly every species of angelfish was reputed to be difficult, if not impossible, to keep in aquaria. The late 1980s and early 1990s changed this for many species. Advances in knowledge about the biology of angelfish, along with comparable advances in aquarium technology and husbandry techniques, meant that some of the former difficult species became more accessible to a larger number of aquarists. The masked angelfish is still a challenging species. Nevertheless, it can now be successfully kept by experienced marine aquarists.

The male masked angelfish *has a golden "mask" and fins. The female's coloration is very different.*

species' natural habitat. If so, the masked angelfish may be more abundant than we currently believe it to be. Even if this were the case, captive breeding may still serve as an important "insurance policy" for the future of the species. It would be a means of providing stocks not just for aquaria but for the restocking of natural habitats should this ever become necessary.

Captive breeding presents a different scale of challenge altogether, and one that has not, as yet, been fully overcome. Successes have been reported for several of the larger species of *Pomacanthus*. However, before masked angelfish can be successfully bred in captivity, further advances need to be made, particularly in relation to the development of appropriate diets for newly hatched fry (young).

Insurance Policy

The masked angelfish is known to be uncommon in the waters around the main Hawaiian islands, where it lives at depths of about 200 feet (60 m). Elsewhere, for example around Kure and Midway Atolls, it has been observed at much shallower depths, and is more common. It is not known if the species is more abundant at depths below 260 feet (75 m), beyond the reach of scuba divers. It could even be that the specimens that are occasionally collected by divers are only those that live at the shallower edge of the

DATA PANEL

Masked angelfish

Genicanthus personatus

Family: Pomacanthidae

World population: Unknown

Distribution: Northwestern islands of the Hawaiian chain

Habitat: Depths of about 60 ft (18 m) downward: (A depth of 275 ft (84 m) has been recorded for 1 specimen.) Often found in open water close to reef drop-offs

Size: Up to 10 in (25 cm) reported for male; perhaps slightly smaller for female

Form: Male: grayish-white body; yellow or yellow-gold "face mask," dorsal (back), pectoral (chest), pelvic (hip), and anal (belly) fins. Caudal (tail) fin has white edge with black vertical band in front half. Topmost and lowermost rays of caudal are extended into filaments. Female: lacks caudal fin extensions, but has the vertical black band.

Dorsal, pectoral, and anal fins are ivory white, as is the body. Pelvic fins have white front half and orange-yellow posterior half. "Face mask" is black

Diet: Mainly zooplankton (minute animal life)

Breeding: No details available, although it is known that females are capable of changing sex. Some other angelfish spawn throughout the summer months, with breeding extending from May–October. Males rise off the bottom and are followed by females; eggs and sperm are released simultaneously into the water. No parental care of the eggs occurs; they float to the water surface and hatch 18–30 hours later into planktonic larvae

Related endangered species: Resplendent pygmy angelfish (*Centropyge resplendens*) LC

Status: Not listed by IUCN

Kure Atoll
Midway Is.
Lisiansk I.
Laysan I.
Gardner & La Perouse Pinnacles
Necker I.
Nihoa
Kauai
Oahu
Maui
Hawaii (UNITED STATES)
Hawaii
Johnston Atoll (U.S.)

Big Scale Archerfish

Toxotes oligolepis

The big scale archerfish is practiced in the art of subterfuge. Skimming silently just under the surface without causing even a ripple, it is a silent, deadly, and lightning-fast predator.

There are six species of archerfish, one of which—the common archerfish—has been popular with aquarists for about 100 years. The big scale archerfish is perhaps the least known of the six. It is one of a small group of remarkable fish belonging to the genus *Toxotes* and is found among the mangroves and freshwater habitats of northern Australia and parts of Asia.

The fish normally feed on flying insects that fall into the water from the air, or from the vegetation in their natural habitat. With their large eyes forever turned skyward, archerfish are always on the lookout for unwary victims that may alight anywhere near the water's surface.

Spitting on Target

When big scale archerfish spot a suitable prey, they simply shoot it down by spitting powerful jets of water at it. The impact knocks the insect off its perch and into the water. Archerfish have also been observed to jump out of the water to seize flying prey. Their aim, while not perfect, is good enough, as evidenced by the large shoals of most species found in their native mangroves.

The water jet is produced by pressing the tongue onto the roof of the mouth, which contains a groove, creating a tube. Closing the gill covers causes a buildup of pressure inside the mouth cavity, which, in turn, forces water into the tube and out of the mouth in the direction of the intended prey.

Remarkable though the shooting down of prey may be, it would be impossible to achieve without the fish's amazing ability to compensate for the refraction (bending) that occurs as light passes from air to water. Refraction causes an object to appear to be where it is not. For example, imagine a straight stick held in front of the body and pointed at an angle to the water's surface, and suppose that the tip of the stick is dipped into the water. The part of the stick that is under the surface will appear to bend upward at an angle to meet the part of the stick held in the hand. The bending is, of course, an illusion; the stick is still perfectly straight, but the water has bent or refracted the rays of light that bounce off the stick (and that allow

DATA PANEL

Big scale archerfish (western archerfish)

Toxotes oligolepis

Family: Toxotidae

World population: Unknown, but abundant within a restricted range

Distribution: Originally reported from the Fitzroy, Isdell, May, and Meda River systems in the Kimberley region of northwestern Australia; also from several streams in Papua New Guinea and Indonesia. Recent reports quote its Australian distribution as just the Fitzroy River extending inland as far as the Geike Gorge National Park

Habitat: Rocky, tree-lined pools

Size: Length: about 6 in (15 cm)

Form: Characteristic archerfish profile of flat back with dorsal (back) fin set well to rear. Body deep and compressed with sharply pointed snout and large, upward-pointing mouth. Eyes large and located on top half of head. Body silvery-white with black blotches or vertical bars. Dorsal, anal (belly), and pelvic (hip) fins are predominantly black, while pectoral (chest) and caudal (tail) fins are transparent

Diet: Takes surface live foods, including insects in aquaria; presumed to feed on similar fare in wild

Breeding: No details available

Related endangered species: None

Status: IUCN LC

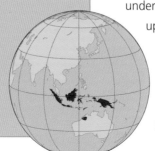

us to see it), creating the impression that the stick is bent.

When archerfish spit at their prey, they have to compensate for the refractive effect, but in reverse, since they are looking upward from the water into the air. They therefore have to shoot "out of true" and hit the target, a feat they manage to execute with impressive regularity.

Cause for Concern?

As a genus, *Toxotes* is not under imminent threat. The big scale archerfish is listed by the IUCN as of lower risk. However, there are some indications that its status could change, since the fish has a fairly restricted geographical range, which could expose it to environmental threats. Recent information about its distribution shows that it occurs in fewer localities within the Australian part of its range. Where it does occur, however, it does so in considerable numbers.

While some of its closest relatives—notably the seven-spot archerfish and the other common archerfish—are reasonably well known, basic information about the big scale archerfish is scarce. This raises questions about its susceptibility to environmental and other disruptive influences. For instance, we do not know what its dietary habits are in any detail, and there are no data on its reproductive biology. In addition, the size of the fish—quoted at up to 6 inches (15 cm)—is only an approximation.

The big scale archerfish is a species that needs to be studied in greater detail. It is also a species that needs to be closely monitored to ensure against the type of crisis that has hit other species, putting them under threat in a remarkably short time.

The big scale archerfish *(inset). Like other archerfish, it stuns its prey with a jet of water that it spits from its mouth; it can hit a target from about 5 feet (1.5 m).*

Bandula Barb

Puntius bandula

The Bandula barb is found in a short stretch of unnamed stream that flows through a number of plantations in Sri Lanka. Now the tiny wild population is under threat of extinction.

Sri Lanka enjoys great riches in terms of freshwater and marine fish species. For many years a large number of these have been highly popular with both scientists and aquarists all around the world. Among the best-known are Sri Lanka's many barbs, some of which, like the black ruby barb, have been intensively bred in captivity and have been developed into a number of varieties with different patterns of colors and fins.

All the island's barb species that are deemed of interest to aquarium keepers have been bred commercially for many years. They include some, like the cherry barb and two-spot barb, that are under threat in the wild. None, though, appear to be under such intense pressure as the Bandula barb.

Inaccessible Fish

Known (but not described) since at least 1980, the Bandula barb has never been collected in any significant numbers. It is found in areas of heavy shade provided by surrounding rubber trees, among the stems of immersed vegetation, or under leaves along the stream margins. Quite simply, other species of barb are more accessible and have been bred so successfully for commercial purposes that the Bandula barb has largely been left alone.

Ranjit Bandula (the scientist after whom the species was named) reports being able to collect up to 100 specimens in one hour during visits between 1980 and 1982. Not long afterward the capture rate plunged to much lower levels. Between 1989 and 1990 another scientist, Rohan Pethiyagoda, made five official visits to collect specimens from which to draw up the scientific description. He collected no specimens at all during heavy rain and a maximum of 14 in the course of one to two hours.

Polluted Waters

One of the key factors leading to the dramatic decline of the Bandula barb appears to be some form of repeated pollution. The cause is probably the runoff from the rice paddy fields that lie upstream of the Bandula barb's preferred waters, and also the rubber plantation through which the stream runs.

DATA PANEL

Bandula barb

Puntius bandula

Family: Cyprinidae

World population: Several thousand in captivity; numbers in wild unknown

Distribution: Sri Lanka: an unnamed stream that flows through Minimaru Coloniya in Pallegama Estate (a rubber plantation) just north of Galapitamada

Habitat: Boulder/pebble-strewn stream with fast-flowing stretches, mud margins, and abundant marginal vegetation

Size: Length: 1.6 in (4.1 cm). Captive-bred specimens are larger

Form: Small, delicately colored fish; light gold with black vertical stripes

Diet: Small invertebrates, detritus, and plant matter; commercial formulations in captivity

Breeding: Eggs scattered mainly among fine-leaved vegetation. Hatching period about 1 day

Related endangered species: Asoka barb *(Puntius asoka)* EN; Two-spot barb *(P. cumingii)* LRcd; black ruby barb *(P. nigrofasciatus)* LRcd; side-striped barb *(B. (P.) pleurotaenia)* LRcd; cherry barb *(B. (P.) titteya)* LRcd; Martenstyn's barb *(B. (P.) martenstyni)* EN

Status: IUCN CR

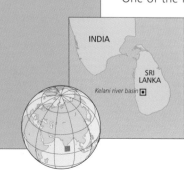

INDIA

SRI LANKA

Kelani river basin

In Search of a New Home

Some time after the collections were made for the official description of the species, a number of specimens were passed to one of Sri Lanka's commercial ornamental fish breeders and exporters to see if the species could be bred in captivity. The breeder has been immensely successful, and there are currently several thousand specimens available for release back into the wild.

There is, however, one major problem in that the small stream that is home to the Bandula barb appears to be under even greater threat than ever before. There is therefore little point in restocking the locality with new fish that would be put at risk of extinction.

The search is on by both the breeder and the island's conservation authorities to find a suitable alternative location. It is, however, not an easy task since any substitute waters are likely to have a complement of species whose natural population balance could be upset by the introduction of what could be termed an "exotic" or nonnative species.

A Precarious Future

The future of the Bandula barb in the wild is poised on a precarious knife edge. On the one hand, the only known wild population could be wiped out overnight if its native stream suffers a major pollution incident. However, there may not be a suitably safe alternative location in the whole of Sri Lanka into which either wild or captive-bred specimens could be released. The one ray of hope is that while efforts to ensure its continued survival in nature continue, stocks are gradually being built up in the relative safety of the fish breeder's facilities.

The Bandula barb *inhabits a short stretch of a minor waterway in Sri Lanka. It breeds well in captivity, but specimens in the wild are susceptible to pollution.*

Mekong Giant Catfish

Pangasianodon gigas

Some of the smallest and largest freshwater fish known to science are catfish. Among the latter there is a toothless, vegetarian giant from the Mekong River—known as the giant catfish. The fish is both sacred and hunted, and its young have not been seen in the wild since the day the species was officially described in 1930.

For a species that has been fished regularly and whose migratory route is firmly established, remarkably little is known about the biology of the giant catfish. Even the validity of its scientific name is in doubt, leading to uncertainty about the true identity of the fish. Some studies indicate that the giant catfish may be better placed in a bigger group: the genus *Pangasius* that contains its closest relatives.

Since numbers of giant catfish in the wild are believed to be small, it could be some time before the situation is resolved. Answers to some of the outstanding questions about the giant catfish's biology and life stages may be provided by studies of captive-bred stocks that are currently being raised for reintroduction into some of the giant catfish's traditional waters.

Search for Clues

The giant catfish—along with its 20 or so *Pangasius* relatives—belongs to the shark catfish family (Pangasiidae). All family members have an elongated body form, a distinctive dorsal (back) fin, an underslung mouth, undulating swimming movements, and an overall passing resemblance in body shape to the true sharks. The Pangasiidae are also closely related to the glass or schilbeid catfish family (Schilbeidae). Some authorities believe that they should each be regarded as a subfamily of a single family rather than as two separate families.

There are two features that set the giant catfish apart from its nearest relatives: the absence of barbels (whiskers) on the lower jaw and the lack of teeth.

It has been observed that in some Pangasius species teeth gradually disappear with age. It is possible that the same applies to the Mekong giant catfish, but since no small or even medium-sized specimens have ever been collected or observed in the wild, the theory is unproven. It has also been proposed that the barbels may be present even in adult specimens, but that they are overgrown by flesh as the jaws become progressively fatter with advancing age. To establish whether or not barbels are

---

DATA PANEL

Giant catfish (Mekong catfish, Thailand giant catfish)

Pangasianodon gigas

Family: Pangasiidae

World population: Low, but exact numbers unknown

Distribution: Mekong River system through Cambodia, Laos, Thailand, Vietnam, and (possibly) part of China

Habitat: Major watercourses and lakes

Size: Length: 6.6–9.8 ft (2–3 m). Weight: 240–660 lb (110–300 kg)

Form: Dorsal (back) profile almost straight; curved belly; flattened head. Lower jaw barbels (whiskers) absent. Large eyes set low on head. Both dorsal and pectoral (chest) fins have prominent spines along front edge; caudal (tail) fin is powerful and forked

Diet: Vegetarian: algae and soft, succulent plants

Breeding: Migrates up to several thousand miles upriver between mid-April and end of May, possibly as far north as Lake Tali in Yunnan, China. Induced spawning in captive-bred specimens has yielded on average 17.6–22 lb (8–10 kg) of eggs

Related endangered species: No close relatives, but Barnard's rock catfish (*Austroglanis barnardi*), in the same order of fish, is Endangered

Status: IUCN CR

present at some stage in the giant catfish's life, juvenile specimens, as well as a series of progressively older ones, would have to be examined.

Threats to Survival

Since so little is known about the life of the Mekong giant catfish, it is impossible to say with any certainty what influence environmental factors have had, or are having, on wild populations. However, it is known that intense fishing over many years brought the species to the brink of extinction. Between 1900–2003 the population in the Mekong River is thought to have declined by 80 percent. The present situation may be a little more hopeful, particularly after the release of some 20,000 young fish from recently established captive-breeding programs into rivers previously inhabited by giant catfish. It is hoped that the captive-bred fish will become established and help sustain the fisheries that exist.

One of the local fisheries has traditionally been associated with Thai New Year festivities during April and May. Coincidentally, it is then that the flesh of the giant catfish is at its tastiest, since the fish have used up much of their body fat during their upstream spawning migration. Perhaps even more important than the actual flavor of the flesh is the belief that

eating giant catfish —or pla buek as it is known locally—leads to a long, healthy, and prosperous life. Add together the two "ingredients" of excellent taste and life-enhancing qualities, and it is easy to understand why the giant catfish commands a high price in Thailand.

Mekong giant catfish have also been fished over the years for oil extraction. Large fish—which can weigh well over 220 pounds (100 kg)—yield correspondingly large quantities of oil. Oil extraction is therefore a worthwhile exercise, despite the fact that wild population levels are low and that fist-sized stones, sometimes found in the stomachs of the giant catfish (perhaps swallowed while feeding on algae-covered rock), wreak havoc with oil-extraction machinery.

An expanding database of information relating to the giant catfish is now emerging. As more is learned about the fish's biology and lifestyle, there will be a greater understanding of how best to conserve the species: Conservationists can use the available data to plan effective strategies for the fish's protection. As current efforts begin to take effect—they include the release of captive-bred specimens and controlled fishing by various fisheries—the fortunes of the giant catfish could be about to take a turn for the better.

The giant catfish *belongs to the shark catfish family and is not unlike a true shark in body shape. The absence of whiskers and teeth in adults distinguishes it from its nearest relatives.*

Alabama Cavefish

Speoplatyrhinus poulsoni

There are probably no more than 100 Alabama cavefish alive today. Such a low number makes the species not just the rarest fish known to science, but also one of the most endangered vertebrates on the planet, teetering between survival and extinction.

The Alabama cavefish is known from just one site: Key Cave on the northern bank of the Tennessee River in Alabama, on the edge of the man-made Pickwick Lake. While the Alabama cavefish may in the past have been more widely distributed, searches carried out in other subterranean waters in the region have failed to yield any specimens. Furthermore, other caves that may have been potential habitats for the cavefish were flooded when Pickwick Lake was created.

As in most caves of any size, conditions within Key Cave remain fairly constant throughout the year, and the animals that live there form an interdependent ecological unit. The cave itself is large and has several levels. In total, some 10,000 feet (3,000 m) of passages have been mapped. The two entrances along Pickwick Lake are major

points of entry and exit to a population of gray bats and other organisms, while permanent Key Cave residents include copepods, amphipods, and isopods (all small crustaceans), as well as some larger crustacea, including three species of crayfish.

Little-Known Species

The Alabama cavefish remains little known because of its extremely low numbers, not just in the wild but in museums as well. There are only nine specimens in collections, and none has, to date, been dissected for gut-content analysis. Cave visits have also yielded little in the way of concrete biological data, since the maximum number of individuals ever observed has never exceeded 10. Much about the cavefish's biology therefore has to be inferred, either from what is known of conditions in Key Cave or from the biology of other, better-known cavefish species.

For example, the Ozark cavefish is known to feed on its own young, and by extrapolation it is thought that the Alabama cavefish may do the same. If this is

DATA PANEL

Alabama cavefish

Speoplatyrhinus poulsoni

Family: Amblyopsidae

World population: Probably less than 100

Distribution: Key Cave on the Tennessee River in Lauderdale County, Alabama

Habitat: Cool-water alkaline pools

Size: Length: 2.8 in (7.2 cm) is the maximum recorded, but larger specimens seen in cave

Form: Eyeless, elongated, pink-bodied fish with flattened head and snout. The head is a third of the body length. Unusually, the anal opening, or vent, is situated forward in throat region. Highly developed lateral line; also sensory papillae on the caudal peduncle (base of tail fin) and along the top and bottom rays of the caudal (tail) fin

Diet: Small aquatic invertebrates, including young crayfish and (possibly) its own offspring

Breeding: Poorly known. Probably fewer than 10% of females breed in any given year. Few eggs are produced, and they, along with the newly hatched larvae, are believed to be incubated within the gill chamber

Related endangered species: Ozark cavefish (*Amblyopsis rosae*) VU; northern cavefish (*A. spelaea*) VU; southern cavefish (*Typhlichthys subterraneus*) VU

Status: IUCN CR

the case, it could offer at least a partial explanation for its low numbers. It is also assumed that the copepods, amphipods, and isopods that inhabit the cave form the other major dietary items, possibly along with juvenile crayfish.

In terms of reproductive strategy the Alabama cavefish may be a gill-chamber brooder, meaning that it may incubate its eggs within a specially enlarged part of the gill chamber. The northern cavefish is known to exhibit such behavior, protecting both its eggs and newly hatched larvae within its similarly adapted gill chambers.

Threats and Recovery

Some of the threats facing the Alabama cavefish are clearcut, the most obvious being its restricted distribution and small population. A less direct but equally important threat comes from the decline of Key Cave's gray bat population. Studies carried out on fish populations in other caves have shown that as the bat populations have declined, so have populations of some other species, most notably those of the southern cavefish. Even though the cavefish does not actually feed on the bats or their droppings, they do rely on aquatic invertebrates that benefit from bat guano (dung).

The existence of the southern cavefish in several caves close to the Alabama cavefish's habitat could also pose a serious threat; indeed, it is possible that

The Alabama cavefish lives in a single cave system on the banks of the Tennessee River. It has no eyes; instead, it senses its way around its dark, subterranean environment.

the southern cavefish may have led to the disappearance of the Alabama cavefish, although no proof has ever come to light. Predation by large crayfish may also present a danger; one species found in Key Cave has been seen to prey on the southern cavefish. Another danger could be groundwater pollution from the surrounding areas, and particularly seepage of chemicals from crop treatments or from a sewage-disposal facility in the nearby city of Florence.

To protect the fish, the Tennessee Valley Authority has fenced off the two entrances to the cave. In addition, constant monitoring of water quality in the region will give rapid warning of any impending crises. If forest, crop, and water-management plans are properly observed, a number of major threats to Key Cave may be averted. Just as important, however, is preserving the health of the gray bat population, which seems to have recovered from a decline of nearly 50 percent between 1969 and 1970.

If all the potential threats are kept in check, the Alabama cavefish may survive. In the meantime, however, a thorough search needs to be put into place in other caves in the region in an attempt to find other, as yet undiscovered populations of this Critically Endangered species.

Blind Cave Characin

Astyanax mexicanus

The blind cave characin is now known to be the same, genetically, as the Mexican tetra. Isolated in three separate cave systems, the fish is vulnerable to many threats.

In 1949 a pink, eyeless fish was imported into Europe. It immediately caused a stir among public aquarium visitors and aquarium keepers. Despite its apparent disability, the fish could find food just as easily as its sighted counterparts. Within a short time it had become popular all over the world. The initial burst of enthusiasm has now diminished, but the blind cave characin continues to attract attention whenever it is exhibited.

Nonidentical Twins

No one could have guessed at the time that the blind cave characin was the same, genetically, as another fish known as the Mexican tetra. At first sight the two fish look so different that they could belong to two distinct species or even, possibly, genera. Yet on closer inspection the underlying similarities soon become apparent. If you ignore the silver, black, and other colors on a Mexican tetra, you end up with a pink fish. Now imagine some fatty tissue over each eye, and the Mexican tetra is transformed into the blind cave characin.

In genetic terms such dramatic differences in appearance can be brought about by relatively minor changes, or mutations, over many generations. The changes are created by being subjected—through natural selection—to the evolutionary pressures of living in caves under conditions of permanent darkness. Studies of genetic material (DNA) carried out on populations of Mexican tetra, both cave or hypogean (those that live belowground) and normal or epigean (those that live aboveground), have confirmed that the Mexican tetra and blind cave characin belong to the same species.

Further proof, if it were needed, occurs in at least one cave in Mexico—Cueva Chica. Periodically, colored and fully sighted Mexican tetras are flushed into the cave when a nearby river floods. Here, in the darkness, they interbreed with their cave counterparts, totally oblivious of their color and eye differences, but able to

DATA PANEL

Blind cave characin (sardina ciega)

Astyanax mexicanus

Family: Characidae

World population: Unknown

Distribution: Mexico, including caves in the Sierras del Abra, de Guatemala, de Perez, and de Colmena

Habitat: Freshwater pools in limestone caves

Size: Length: 3.5 in (9 cm)

Form: Pink, eyeless fish; reduced scales; anal fin is completely straight in females but convex in males

Diet: Wide-ranging; includes bat droppings, other fish, and eggs

Breeding: Slightly adhesive eggs are scattered over substratum and abandoned (parents may consume own eggs). Hatching takes about 1 day at about 75°F (24°C); may take up to 3 days at lower temperatures; newborn fish (fry) become

free-swimming 3 days later

Related endangered species: None, but some epigean (aboveground) populations of *Astyanaz mexicanus* are known to be declining. In the same family the naked characin (*Gymnocharacinus bergii*) of Argentina is Endangered

Status: IUCN VU

respond to all the other cues that identify each to the other as belonging to one and the same species.

Records of interbreeding between river and cave populations were being made as far back as 1942, but it took many years for the knowledge to become accepted universally. Even then, two different scientific names persisted until constant repetition brought the necessary shift toward uniformity.

Lurking Threats

The blind cave characin has a restricted distribution and is native to just three main cave systems. The caves are completely separated from each other, which means that populations are isolated. Hence the status of the cave populations is clearly of concern. In such diverse and complicated water systems the threat of pollution can never be totally discounted. Neither can the effects of extended droughts in the region, which can result in dangerous lowering of water levels in the pools inhabited by the cave fish. Pumping of the cave water for irrigation purposes also lowers water levels. In addition, more widespread hybridization between the aboveground and belowground types could lead to a dilution of "cave characteristics" in at least some populations.

Overall, the future of the blind cave characin is insecure. Any of the above factors—all of which are avoidable—could in a short time render the fish Critically Endangered or Extinct in its native habitat. A drop in water level would be one of the quickest routes to extinction. In the event of such a disaster fish bred commercially for the aquarium trade could be used to replace the wild communities, but only if their native habitats were deemed suitable for restocking.

The blind cave characin *lacks any body pigment and has only fat-covered, vestigial eyes, unlike the Mexican tetra (inset). Despite looking completely different and living in separate habitats, the two are genetically almost identical.*

Atlantic Cod

Gadus morhua

Whether freshly caught, deep-frozen, smoked, or dried and salted, the Atlantic cod is a familiar food in Europe and North America. Fishing, intensified to new levels with trawlers developed over the last few decades, has severely depleted stocks of the once-abundant fish.

Atlantic cod have occurred in vast numbers over their extensive range, making them accessible to commercial fisheries in many countries. The species is considered a prime food fish, and its liver is the source of cod-liver oil, a substance rich in vitamins A and D that is used widely as a vitamin supplement. However, evidence suggests that the fish are in greater danger than anyone would have thought. It is also possible that the early years of the 21st century will be, in retrospect, the swan song of the traditional British dish of (cod) fish and chips (fries).

DATA PANEL

Atlantic cod (northern cod)

Gadus morhua

Family: Gadidae

World population: Low enough to be considered vulnerable. Newfoundland catch rose from about 1,700 tons in 1994 to 2,700 tons in 2006

Distribution: North Atlantic

Habitat: Juveniles live just below the lower tidal zone to about 66 ft (20 m); adults found from 66 ft (20 m) down to 260 ft (80 m): may occur at 1,970 ft (600 m)

Size: Length: 30–70 in (80–180 cm). Weight: 80–211 lb (36–96 kg)

Form: Stout but streamlined fish. Well-developed barbel (whisker) on chin, 3 dorsal (back) and 2 anal (belly) fins. Coloration variable: may be olive-brown or greenish on the back, shading into lighter tones toward the belly: belly is whitish. The base color is overlaid with numerous dark spots

Diet: A bottom-feeder with a strong preference for mollusks, crustacea, worms, and smaller fish

Breeding: Spawns February–April/May at about 660 ft (200 m). In some areas, such as the North Sea, spawning may take place at 66–330 ft (20–100 m). Up to 9 million eggs released by a large female. Eggs and larvae are left to fend for themselves

Related endangered species: Haddock (*Melanogrammus aeglefinus*) VU

Status: IUCN VU

Prolific Migrants

Young cod (codlings) congregate in shallow water, which can extend from close to the low tidal zone to a depth of about 66 feet (20 m). As they mature, these juveniles tend to frequent a much wider range of water depths, moving between 66 and 260 feet (20 and 80 m). Cod can, however, be found at much deeper levels than this, however; some reportedly occur at depths of between 1,640 and 1,970 feet (500 and 600 m).

In terms of temperature tolerance the Atlantic cod is just as versatile and adaptable. Although it prefers water that is between 39 and 45°F (4 to 7°C), it can be found at temperatures of 25 to 61°F (-4 to 16°C). Such tolerance is essential for a species that is a bottom-feeder but whose feeding depth varies widely.

Cod congregate in great shoals (groups of fish) and undertake lengthy migrations to reach their spawning grounds. There the males go through an elaborate courtship dance, involving extending their fins and twisting and turning. A large female cod can produce over 9 million eggs, but the chances of any individual egg or larva surviving are small.

The Great Cod Collapse

In the 19th century, when areas of the North Atlantic were first fished, cod were both abundant and, on average, much larger than today. Some cod weighing up to 200 pounds (90 kg) were recorded. Now, after years of intensive fishing, even a cod of 40 pounds (18 kg) is considered large.

The Atlantic cod *has a long, tapering body with three dorsal (back) fins. It has long been considered a prime food fish.*

Up until the 1950s annual catches (which averaged about 400 million cod) seemed to have no significant effect on population levels. Then came the factory trawlers, with gigantic nets and onboard processing and freezing facilities. During the mid-1950s and 1960s catches rose dramatically. Some 800,000 tons were caught in the Northwest Atlantic in 1968. Soon, however, catches began to drop just as quickly. The situation in the Canadian fishing grounds deteriorated to the point were factory trawlers were excluded from fishing the waters. The domestic fleet continued to fish, but catches were lower.

In the late 1970s the new-generation factory trawlers arrived—the so-called draggers. Their nets trapped huge numbers of fish, but they also plowed up the bottom, destabilizing and destroying the habitats on which the cod and numerous other species depended for their survival. Added to this (although the point is hotly debated), heavy predation by fast-expanding seal populations may have contributed further to the decline in stocks that followed. To make matters worse, delays in implementing scientific recommendations led to severe depletion of cod throughout the Canadian fishing grounds. In 1992 a total ban was imposed on cod fishing around Newfoundland, with further restrictions following in other cod-fishing areas. Thousands of people lost their jobs, and the fishing industry was plunged into crisis. The restrictions were relaxed in 2006.

In 2001 the European Union ordered a ban on all deep-sea fishing in more than 40,000 square miles (104,000 sq. km) of the North Sea—the area of the Atlantic between Britain and the Northern European mainland—to prevent the collapse of cod stocks there. And in 2011 the European Union reduced the amount of fish that could be caught off Scotland and Ireland by 25 percent. It remains to be seen whether fishing controls will guarantee the survival of the Atlantic cod.

Mountain Blackside Dace

Phoxinus cumberlandensis

Restricted to a few streams in the Cumberland River drainage system in Kentucky and northeastern Tennessee, the mountain blackside dace is threatened on several fronts. Habitat alteration as a direct result of logging, mining, and road construction has contributed to competition with other species and resulted in reduced populations.

The first specimens of the mountain blackside dace were collected in 1975 within the Daniel Boone National Forest. Because they were colored the same as other *Phoxinus* species, little attention was paid to the specimens, although they came from a small area where dace populations had not been studied before. It took three more years for the differences between the mountain blackside dace and its closest relatives to be fully appreciated. Since then a great deal has been learned about the fish.

DATA PANEL

Mountain blackside dace

Phoxinus cumberlandensis

Family: Cyprinidae

World population: Unknown

Distribution: Short stretches of streams in Cumberland River drainage system of southeastern Kentucky and northeastern Tennessee

Habitat: Silt-free pools in upper reaches of streams where there is a flow of cool running water. Substratum of sand, gravel, pebbles, and rocks. Undercut banks, particularly shaded by overlapping vegetation

Size: Length: 2.8 in (7.2 cm)

Form: Slim-bodied fish with pointed snout and short, robust fins. Black stripe runs from snout, through eye, and along body, ending at caudal peduncle (base of tail). In mature male the chin/throat area, "neck," and whole of underside of body are red,

especially during breeding season. Base of dorsal (back) fin is also red. Rest of fins are dusky gold or yellow, while top half of body is olive gold

Diet: Mainly algae, detritus, and small aquatic invertebrates

Breeding: In April–June males gather at silt-free nest sites and await the arrival of a female. When one arrives, groups of males swarm around her and spawn with her. Little else is known, but the young are believed to mature in 1 year. Life span between 3 and 4 years

Related endangered species: Tennessee dace (*Phoxinus tennesseensis*) LRnt

Status: IUCN VU

Silt-Sensitive

Of particular interest is the mountain blackside dace's sensitivity to silt-laden water, a characteristic that restricts it to clear-water areas of streams—especially pools of about 39 inches (100 cm) depth—fed by flowing water from narrower, shallower stretches. Such pools contain undercut banks and dense surrounding vegetation. The substratum can be sandy, gravelly, or rocky, but is free of fine sediments. Most pools are located at altitudes of about 900 to 1,600 feet (275 to 490 m) above sea level.

The mountain blackside dace exhibits coloration like that of several other species in the genus *Phoxinus*, in which the males in particular display brilliantly during the breeding season.

Short-Stretch Distribution

Although no proof is available at the moment, there is a possibility that in the past the mountain blackside dace may have occurred in well over 50 other streams within the Cumberland River system. Populations are currently only known from about 30 streams in the upper reaches of the system. In addition, of the known populations 27 are restricted to stretches of water of about 1 mile (1.5 km) or less. Some are actually found within stretches of only a few hundred yards. The mountain blackside dace must be considered significantly at risk, since all the streams are located within a relatively small area and so could be altered by the same environmental factors.

Few species of fish apart from the mountain blackside dace are found in these waters. However, one that is sometimes encountered is the southern redbelly dace. An interesting relationship exists between the two species with dominance seemingly determined by water flow. Where water flow is relatively high, resulting in clear, sediment-free water, the mountain blackside dace tends to outnumber its relative. However, where this flow has been reduced—for example, by alteration of the stream gradient—the southern redbelly assumes dominance, sometimes to the extent that it totally replaces the mountain blackside dace over a period of time.

This dynamic relationship was discovered not long after the mountain blackside dace was recognized as a separate species. It provided a clear early warning signal that the species could be placed under serious threat by a competitor that was able to exploit slow-water conditions to its advantage.

Decline and Recovery

The main problem facing the mountain blackside dace is changes in ambient conditions—which can include a rise in water temperature—to favor the southern redbelly dace. The higher suspended silt content of the water in altered habitats is obviously significant. As a consequence, the southern redbelly—along with other species like the bluntnose minnow—not only finds a foothold alongside the mountain blackside dace, but also competes with it for available food resources.

A further threat comes from coal mines in the area. Strip mining in particular has resulted in heavy siltation, as well as acidic runoff, and the two factors together have caused declines in the mountain blackside dace populations in affected streams. Whether or not modern coal-mining techniques are still having the same effect is not clear at the moment.

Logging, road construction, and other habitat-altering activities within the species' range have also had (and are still having) a negative effect on population levels. A study carried out in the mid-1980s indicated that the combined effects of all these factors had led to a situation where only nine of the 30 known habitats contained healthy mountain blackside dace populations.

To what extent, if any, the species has recovered or declined further in the locations in recent years is not known. The key to its survival in its native waters undoubtedly lies in adequate monitoring and control of the habitat-altering and habitat-degrading factors that so easily affect its populations.

Mountain blackside dace *exhibit colors like their relatives'—red, black, white or silver, and dusky gold.*

Lesser Spiny Eel

Macrognathus aral

The lesser spiny eel is relatively abundant in India, but populations have severely declined in Sri Lanka, where it is now only found in four locations. The reasons for the population decline are not known, and neither is the potential threat to other spiny eel populations elsewhere.

The only thing that spiny eels have in common with the "true" eels is their cylindrical and elongated body shape. Otherwise, they are quite different. True eels (family Anguillidae of the order Anguilliformes) are long, slender fish known for the long-distance migrations undertaken by at least two species—the North American eel and the European eel—to and from their spawning grounds. Although they are freshwater eels, they spawn in the Sargasso Sea, a calm area in the North Atlantic between the West Indies and the Azores. True eels produce leptocephali—slender, transparent larvae that do not resemble adults. They gradually undergo metamorphosis to juveniles on their journey back to freshwater rivers. On reaching maturity years later, they return to the Sargasso Sea to spawn.

Unlike true eels, spiny eels are freshwater fish that live, breed, and die in rivers. Their larvae do not go through the leptocephalus stage; young spiny eels are tiny replicas of their parents.

There are two groups of fish known as spiny eels: the freshwater fish of the family Mastacembelidae and the deep-sea fish of the family Notacanthidae—a little-known group. In the Mastacembelidae, which includes the lesser spiny eel, there are about 70 species in four genera. Two genera—namely *Aethiomastacembelus* and *Caecomastacembelus* (sometimes called *Afromastacembelus*)—are found in Africa, and the other two—*Mastacembelus* and *Macrognathus*—are found in Asia.

The common name of spiny eels reflects the series of small spines that extend for varying distances along

DATA PANEL

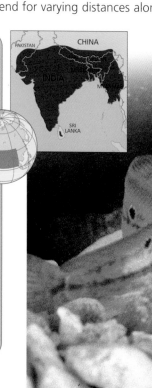

Lesser spiny eel

Macrognathus aral

Family: Mastacembelidae

World population: Relatively abundant in parts of its range, but close to extinction (or extinct) in Sri Lanka

Distribution: Indian subcontinent, Myanmar (Burma), and Sri Lanka

Habitat: Mainly still or slow-flowing waters with marginal vegetation and muddy or silty bottoms

Size: Length: up to 12 in (30 cm) reported

Form: Elongated, slender body with series of small, isolated spines running down the back up to the front edge of the soft part of the dorsal (back) fin. Snout tapered, ending in 3 fleshy lobes. Dorsal

(back), caudal (tail), and anal (belly) fins are separate (they are fused in some other spiny eels); there are no pelvic (hip) fins. Two brown stripes separated by yellowy stripes run the length of the body; dorsal fin has 2 or more ocelli (eyelike markings): black spots edged in yellow

Diet: Aquatic insects and other invertebrates

Breeding: Little is known about courtship and breeding behavior. Eggs are laid on vegetation and apparently abandoned. Hatching takes place in 1 or 2 days

Related endangered species: None

Status: IUCN LC

the back and up to the front edge of the soft part of the dorsal (back) fin. These are used in defense when a fish feels threatened. Some species, for instance, will wriggle backward when picked up, giving the handler a nasty and painful surprise with the spines. The backward movement is probably an instinctive reaction that in the wild would allow the fish to bury itself rapidly in the soft mud or silt on the riverbed and so escape from danger.

Abundant or Endangered?

General information about the family of spiny eels is readily available, but detailed data on many species, including the lesser spiny eel, is more difficult to find. It is known that the species is relatively abundant on the Indian subcontinent and in Myanmar (Burma). Indeed, Indian specimens are regularly exported for home aquaria and are reported to be "ideal aquarium inhabitants." Along with other members of the family, the lesser spiny eel is considered a delicious food in India, and at one time it was also thought to be a delicacy in Sri Lanka.

The collapse of Sri Lanka's lesser spiny eel population has led to a growing belief that it could be extinct in this part of its range. However, occasional reports in recent years have located isolated specimens at a few sites, which suggests that the "extinct" label may be a little premature. In 1991 researchers reported that they had found the species in four locations. Since sightings do occur, the species is regarded as rare rather than extinct. Nevertheless, the lesser spiny eel was once abundant enough for it to be collected from rice paddies or even on baited hook and line.

Equally worrying is the fact that the cause, or causes, of the decline in the populations is unknown. There are no indications that overcollection for consumption or home aquaria is a contributory factor. On the other hand, the use of pesticides in farming and changes brought about through agriculture are thought to have been detrimental to the eel's habitat. However, no detailed studies have been carried out.

It is clear that the lesser spiny eel is in a precarious state. While the species as a whole is not under threat, the Sri Lankan population undoubtedly is. Since the decline has been so dramatic and is so little understood, it raises questions about the long-term stability of the other lesser spiny eel populations.

The lesser spiny eel *resembles the true eel, but is not related to it. It is an elongated fish that is nocturnal and burrows in the riverbed during most of the day.*

EX

EW

CR

EN

VU

NT

LC

O

Australian Lungfish

Neoceratodus forsteri

Fish breathe through their gills; land-based animals use their lungs. However, the division is not as clearcut as it might appear. Some can use other parts of the body for respiration as well, such as a special organ in the gill chamber, parts of the gut, or (like the Australian lungfish) a lung.

The Australian lungfish, along with its closest relatives, the African and South American lungfish, is regarded as a primitive animal: There is even some doubt as to whether it is really a fish at all. Evidence includes the fact that some species have characteristics that indicate similarities with amphibians. They include external gills during the larval stages, limblike pectoral and pelvic fins, the continuous dorsal (back), caudal (tail), and anal (belly) fins, the large heavy-duty body scales, and lungs.

Australian Differences

The Australian, or Queensland, lungfish, while sharing many characteristics with its African and South American cousins, differs from them in significant ways. The most fishlike of all the species, its fins look more like fins than underdeveloped legs. Its newly hatched larvae also lack the amphibianlike external gills present in the young of other species, although at first they still look more like tadpoles than baby fish.

One important difference relates to the lungs. Other lungfish have two such structures consisting of extensions of the esophagus (gullet) that run along the top of the abdominal cavity, roughly in the same position as the swim-bladder in "normal" fish. In the Australian lungfish, while the arrangement is similar, there is only one lung.

Another difference relates to summer survival. All lungfish are able to supplement their gill breathing by taking atmospheric air into their lungs at the water surface. They are also capable of tolerating unfavorable (oxygen-deficient) water conditions that would kill most other fish. In the African and South American species this survival capacity is taken a step further. Not only can the lungfish survive very low-oxygen water conditions, they can even survive periods of drought when the pools in which they live dry out completely.

As the drying out process goes on, the fish burrow into the bottom mud, secrete a mucous "cocoon" or chamber (the South American lungfish does not line its chamber with mucus), and go into a state of estivation (dormancy) until the arrival of the next rains. The Australian lungfish does not have this ability and will die if its native waters dry out. Nevertheless, its survival capabilities are resilient enough to allow at least some individuals to survive a few days out of water as long as they are in the shade, and their body remains moist.

Ancient Lineage

The history of lungfish can be traced back through the fossil record. Fossils of the Australian type of lungfish have been found in Triassic rocks (about 203 million years old). Fossil cocoons, or burrows—sometimes with a lungfish inside—have been found in Permian and Carboniferous rocks (270 and 350 million years old, respectively). However, the heyday of lungfish appears to have been during the Devonian period—from about 350 to 400 million years ago. Fossils of lungfish that are apparently identical to modern-day Australian lungfish have been found in rocks about 100 million years old in New South Wales. The Australian lungfish is recognized as the oldest known species of fish today. Consequently, it enjoys the status of "living fossil."

Australian lungfish *have an ancient lineage that can be traced through the fossil record over millions of years.*

Threatened or Not?

Undoubtedly, all lungfish are fascinating from the biological point of view, and the Australian lungfish is no exception. It has therefore been studied in great detail, and its distribution is well documented. We know as a result of these studies that lungfish were once widely distributed throughout Australia. Today, however, the species is only found naturally in southeastern Queensland, within the Burnett and Mary river systems. Over the years it has also been introduced into other southeastern Queensland waters, some of which are now known to hold self-sustaining populations.

While this restricted distribution may appear to justify concern about the ongoing survival of the species, informed opinion seems to be reasonably confident that the Australian lungfish is no longer heading for extinction. Today, probably as a result of the protection it receives, populations are on the increase, which bodes well for its future.

DATA PANEL

Australian lungfish

Neoceratodus forsteri

Family: Ceratodidae

World population: Numbers believed to be relatively high within the range. Some introduced populations are self-sustaining

Distribution: Naturally occurring in the Mary and Burnett river systems of southeastern Queensland, Australia. Introduced into other watercourses and into some reservoirs in Queensland and northern New South Wales

Habitat: Still pools or other bodies of deep, slow-flowing water, which are susceptible to seasonal fluctuations in water level, clarity, and quality

Size: Length: up to 5 ft (1.5 m). Weight: 88 lb (40 kg)

Form: Sturdy, but elongated body; paddlelike pectoral (chest) and pelvic (hip) fins. Dorsal (back), caudal (tail), and anal (belly) fins are continuous. Body scales are stout, large, round, and overlapping. Eyes are small in relation to body. Coloration olive-green or gray-brown on back and down sides, but white on underside of head and along belly; scattering of dark irregular spots adorns side of body in many specimens, increasing in abundance toward the tail

Diet: Aquatic vertebrates and invertebrates; also aquatic vegetation

Breeding: Spawning season August–December with peak activity in October. Usually occurs at night among submerged vegetation at temperatures of 68–77°F (20–25°C). Eggs laid during a period of about 1 hour and then apparently abandoned. Hatching occurs 3 weeks later. Growth of larvae is slow, and it is not known at what age or size maturity is reached. Life span up to 50 years

Related endangered species: None

Status: IUCN LC

Queensland

AUSTRALIA

New South Wales

Paddlefish

Polyodon spathula

The paddlefish, with its distinctive, paddlelike snout, is one of the strangest-looking fish in the world. It is also a source of caviar—the expensive delicacy made from salted roe (eggs), usually of the sturgeon fish.

The paddlefish is a substantial animal with an equally substantial appetite. Like other large predators such as the whale shark and its relative, the basking shark, it does not hunt down and kill large prey. Instead, it feeds by swimming through "clouds" of plankton with its mouth open, straining out the tiny organisms with its sievelike gill rakers.

Paddle Purpose

The paddle (rostrum, or beaklike part) of the fish accounts for almost a third of its body length, and its exact function is still a mystery. It has long been thought to play a fundamentally important role during feeding, and some experts believe it to be a tool that the fish uses to stir up the mud. That is probably not the case since the paddlefish's main food source is freeswimming microscopic invertebrates. It is more likely that the rich supply of sensory cells in the paddle helps the fish detect and locate its food. It could also act as a stabilizer when the fish swims with its cavernous mouth open. However, it has been noted that when a paddlefish has lost part or the whole of the paddle through injury, it can still detect food and feed adequately.

Ancient Relationships

Fossil evidence shows that paddlefish have existed since the the Cretaceous and Eocene periods (about 135 million years ago) when dinosaurs existed. Like the primitive marine bony fish the coelacanth, they are regarded as "living fossils." The paddlefish's long operculi (gill covers) are probably a primitive feature.

Paddlefish have a skeleton made of cartilage (a tough, elastic tissue), like sharks, although the jaw is made of bone. The caudal (tail) fin is also sharklike, having a long top lobe. The skin is virtually scaleless

DATA PANEL

American paddlefish (duckbill cat, shovelfish, spadefish, spoonbill)

Polyodon spathula

Family: Polyodontidae

World population: More than 10,000 mature individuals

Distribution: Mainly Mississippi River Basin and Gulf Slope drainage, U.S.

Habitat: Slow-flowing waters; prefer oxbow lakes and backwaters where the depth exceeds about 4 ft (1.2 m)

Size: Length: up to 6.6 ft (2 m). Mature females larger than males. Weight: over 100 lb (45 kg)

Form: Elongated body; sharklike with rostrum (paddlelike snout). Slate colored, often mottled, with lighter shading in the lower half

Diet: Small invertebrates (zooplankton) and insect larvae

Breeding: Spawning in April and May at water temperatures of about 55°F (13°C). Females can produce about 7,500 eggs per 1 lb (450 g) of body weight. The large eggs hatch in about a week and the fry are free-swimming. Juveniles grow at a rate of 1 in (2.5 cm) per week. Females mature at 10 years. Life span 30 years

Related endangered species: Chinese paddlefish (*Psephurus gladius*) CR

Status: IUCN VU

and the jaws toothless, although young specimens have numerous tiny teeth that they gradually lose as they mature. Young are born without a paddle.

Today paddlefish have few living relatives; the closest are the 25 species of sturgeon, with which they share the order Acipenseriformes.

Threats to Survival

Paddlefish were once common in their native waters, but habitat alteration, reduced water quality, and overfishing all led to a significant decrease in numbers.

Habitat alteration has been of two major types: watercourse channelization and dam building. Both have deprived the paddlefish of essential feeding and spawning areas. Water degradation has occurred primarily as a result of pollution, while overfishing has been largely illegal and relatively recent.

Stocks are now on the increase in some parts of the species' original range. However, a sharp decline in paddlefish numbers occurred as a result of overfishing during the 1980s, when sturgeon from Iran were unavailable—Iran was fighting a war. Paddlefish were then poached to make up the shortfall.

The American paddlefish *is greenish gray and inhabits the Mississippi Basin. The other species, the larger Chinese paddlefish, inhabits the Yangtse River Basin.*

Conserving Stocks

Where the paddlefish is fairly abundant, it is fished on a strict quota basis; it is hoped that this will lead to sustainable natural stocks. In many inland waters, as well as the paddlefish's traditional stronghold, the Mississippi River, fishing continues all year round but only allows a maximum catch of two fish per day. On the Missouri River there is no open season.

Running alongside such measures, a number of hatchery-based programs—set up in the early 1990s—produced thousands of juveniles for restocking. Tagging of many of the hatchery-raised juveniles is leading to greater understanding of the species. It will, however, be several years before we know how successful these fish are at reproducing in the wild.

Ornate Paradisefish

Malpulutta kretseri

The ornate paradisefish is found in streams deep in the jungle of southwestern Sri Lanka. It is a tiny, bubble-blowing jewel of a fish whose numbers are low in the wild. Since 1998 it has been protected in a unique agreement between the island authorities and ornamental aquatic industry.

The IUCN lists the ornate paradisefish as Lower Risk, conservation dependent. In this situation remedial action is usually taken to save a species from becoming Vulnerable or Endangered. In the case of the ornate paradisefish, however, it is not known why numbers are low in the wild. Indeed, it is possible that its scarcity does not indicate a declining population at all; instead, it may represent longstanding stability. Evidence seems to suggest that the fish is perhaps even more abundant today than it was in the past. Nonetheless, in Sri Lanka the species is regarded as Uncommon, Threatened, or Endangered.

Pollution can largely be discounted as a reason for the low population size since the fish inhabits remote forest streams, far away from human activities. Overcollection can also be ruled out, since there is not a great demand for ornate paradisefish by aquarists,

despite its undoubted beauty. Specialized hobbyists who concentrate on anabantoids (labyrinth fish) have in the past bought small numbers of wild-caught ornate paradisefish. However, today's (still limited) supply comes from the aquarium-bred offspring of these original specimens. The fish are often exchanged between members of anabantoid-keeping and breeding associations or sold to local specialized aquatic outlets.

Some authorities believe that the two known forms of ornate paradisefish—distinguishable by their color—in fact represent separate subspecies: *Malpulutta kretseri kretseri* (inhabiting the Bentota Basin) and *Malpulutta kretseri minor* (a form with blue fin edges, found in the Kalu Basin). There is also a violet-colored variant.

Bubble-Nest Breeding

The paradisefish has fascinating breeding behavior. As in many other labyrinth fish (freshwater spiny-finned fish with a special respiratory organ), the male builds a

---

DATA PANEL

Ornate paradisefish

Malpulutta kretseri

Family: Belontiidae

World population: Unknown

Distribution: Southwestern Sri Lanka: Colombo-Galle-Ratnapura triangle

Habitat: Small, shady, shallow streams—often silted and containing abundant submerged leaf debris—in forested areas

Size: Up to 2.4 in (6 cm) reported, but wild-caught specimens average only 0.8 in (2 cm)

Form: Tiny labyrinth fish; brilliantly colored scales. Male's coloration intensifies during mating displays. Breathes air with use of auxiliary respiratory organ

Diet: Small aquatic invertebrates

Breeding: Male builds bubble-nest and attracts female to it; spawning embraces occur, and up to 200 eggs are laid. Male guards eggs until they hatch (2 days). Hatchlings are free-swimming after 3–5 days

Related endangered species: Combtail *(Belontia signata)* LRcd

Status: IUCN LRcd

The ornate paradisefish *is a tiny, colorful, air-breathing fish that is only found in the shady jungle streams of southwestern Sri Lanka, where it is protected.*

nest of mucus-covered bubbles under a submerged leaf or, occasionally, in a sheltered spot on the surface of a shallow pool. Following a long series of impressive displays during which the male extends his fins and intensifies his brilliant coloration, the pair repeatedly embrace under the bubbles. When the female releases each small batch of eggs, they are immediately fertilized by the male. The pair (but more often the female) then gather the sinking eggs in their mouths and blow them into the bubble-nest. The procedure is repeated until between 100 and 200 eggs are laid over a period of time, which can be as short as one hour or as long as 12 hours. Once all the eggs are laid, the female leaves, and the male stands guard until the eggs hatch about two days later. The fry (young fish) become free-swimming some three to five days after hatching

Securing a Future

In 1998 continuing concern about the relatively low abundance of the species in the wild led to a resolution: Sri Lanka's ornamental fish exporters and the island's authorities agreed to ban exportation of all wild-caught specimens. Instead, permission was granted for small numbers of paradisefish to be collected from several localities and for captive-breeding programs to be established using the specimens as breeding stock.

In order to get the program successfully underway, and to avoid some of the major difficulties of breeding such a challenging species, the Anabantoid Association of Great Britain contributed data that had been collected from members with direct experience in spawning paradisefish in aquariums. Within a few months the first success was reported. Others followed soon after, indicating that the future of this tiny labyrinth fish may now be reasonably secure.

Knysna Seahorse

Hippocampus capensis

With their miniature bony-plated bodies, curled tails, and horselike heads, seahorses are distinctive in their appearance and remarkable in many other ways. Seahorses are harvested for the souvenir trade, but the Knysna seahorse is also threatened by the effects of tourism on its native habitat.

Seahorses are unusual fish, partly because of their armor-plated bodies and their upright swimming position. They lack the caudal (tail) fin that we normally associate with fish. Instead, there is a true tail that can be curled up and extended almost like the prehensile (adapted for grasping) tail of a monkey or a chameleon. Seahorses use their tails to cling onto vegetation and other objects, or even each other. Camouflage is another property that seahorses have that distinguishes them from many other fish. As well as being able to change color, seahorses can also develop elongations and other skin growths that allow them to blend in so effectively with their surroundings that they can become virtually invisible. This ability is best seen in seahorse species usually referred to as sea dragons (*Phycodorus eques* and *Phyllopteryx taeniolatus*), which are covered with outgrowths that look remarkably like seaweed. Another unusual characteristic of seahorses is that they are monogamous. Monogamy—the pairing up of a male and female for life or, as in the case of seahorses, for a breeding season or more—is not a trait that is normally encountered among fish.

Most amazing of all are the seahorse's breeding habits. In a total reversal of what we find in other animals, it is the male seahorse that incubates the eggs. Following an intricate courtship ritual, the pair face each other, and the female releases a batch of eggs into the male's abdominal brood pouch. Further batches are added to the original one until anything from 50 to 1,500 eggs (depending on the species) have been produced. They are later self-fertilized by the males. Parental duties become the exclusive responsibility of the male, which incubates the eggs. Once these eggs are ready to hatch, the male goes through a series of convulsions and contractions, gradually releasing the tiny juvenile seahorses, which are left to fend for themselves.

DATA PANEL

Knysna seahorse (Cape seahorse)

Hippocampus capensis

Family: Syngnathidae

World population: A few hundred

Distribution: Knysna Estuary, Cape Province, South Africa; also in a few bays in the surrounding region

Habitat: Submerged estuarine meadows ranging in depth from about 20 in–66 ft (50 cm–20 m)

Size: Length: 2–4.3 in (5–11 cm)

Form: Bony-plated body and horselike head with tubular snout (short in comparison to nearest relatives). Forward-curled tails. Coloration greenish or brownish, usually mottled; may also have dark body spots. Lacks the coronet (crownlike structure on top of the head) found in many other seahorse species

Diet: Small aquatic invertebrates

Breeding: Repeated matings and broods between September and April at water temperatures above 68°F (20°C). Female releases batches of eggs into male's abdominal pouch; eggs are self-fertilized by the male; male gives birth to 7–95 fry (young) after gestation period of 14–21 days. Maturity is reached in about 1 year

Related endangered species: Thirty-five species of seahorse, sea dragon, and pipe fish (all members of the family Syngnathidae) are listed as Vulnerable by the IUCN; 7 are listed as Data Deficient

Status: IUCN EN

Trade in Seahorses

No fewer than 46 countries and regions are involved in the seahorse trade, with annual exports from the main suppliers ranging from 3 to 15 tons. Even if these figures were to relate to live "fresh" or deep-frozen seahorses, the actual numbers of specimens involved would be colossal. When we consider that the data relate to dried specimens, which are only a fraction of the weight of live ones, the weights translate into many millions of individual seahorses.

Seahorses are thought by some Asian communities—particularly but not exclusively the Chinese—to be able to cure a host of illnesses and Traditional Chinese medicine undoubtedly accounts for much of the world demand for the animals.

The souvenir trade is also a large-scale consumer of seahorses. They are sold as dried and varnished specimens and made into a host of small decorative objects such as keyrings, paperweights, and so on.

Collections of live specimens for home aquaria also play a part in the seahorse trade. Even conservative estimates show that collecting could represent a significant additional pressure on wild populations of many species of seahorse.

In the case of the Knysna seahorse, which is found west of Port Elizabeth in Cape Province, South Africa, collection for the souvenir trade and aquaria does not appear to be the major cause of decline. Tourism and pollution, however, have put the species at risk. Tourism is responsible for creating pressure on the estuary around Knysna Lagoon, where freshwater floods have caused heavy mortalities among the resident seahorse population. Increasing levels of pollution mean that even captive-bred specimens cannot be released into their home waters.

The damaging effects of tourism, allied to the restricted range of the species and its extreme rarity, led to the Knysna seahorse being classified by the IUCN as Endangered in 1996.

Seahorses *are weak swimmers. They cling to seaweed and propel themselves along with their fins, rising and falling by altering the amount of air in their swim-bladders. The Knysna seahorse lacks the crownlike structure on the top of the head that is found in many other species.*

Conservation

Research studies on wild populations are seen as a vital step in establishing the actual status of seahorse species around the world. A major industry-backed project, the Global Marine Aquarium Database, launched in 2000, should help identify the main species that are traded, assisting in the establishment of sustainable harvesting policies and identifying which species may be in need of protection.

Captive breeding of the Knysna seahorse has been undertaken using adult specimens supplied by the South African government. Attempts are also being made to control conditions in the natural habitat; if successful, the release of captive-bred specimens into their home waters may be possible.

Spring Pygmy Sunfish

Elassoma alabamae

True to its name, the spring pygmy sunfish is tiny. It lives among dense vegetation and is often hard to find. Yet it has received an enormous amount of interest over the years, mainly because for about three decades it was believed to be extinct.

Although pygmy sunfish have been known and studied for well over 100 years, their relationship with their presumed close cousins, the much larger sunfish (family Centrarchidae), has been the focus of considerable controversy. The closeness of their kinship—and whether it is close enough for them to be regarded as members of the same family—has been hotly disputed ever since the first species, the banded pygmy sunfish, was described by scientists in 1877.

Currently, size and skeletal differences between the two groups are generally accepted as being marked enough for the pygmies to have their own family, the Elassomatidae, consisting of just six species. However, new evidence now seems to indicate that the relationship between the pygmy sunfish and the other sunfish may not be close at all;

they could even be more closely related to sticklebacks and swamp eels instead. It appears, therefore, that new controversies lie ahead.

Limited Distribution

In 1937 a scientific collection at Cave Spring in Lauderdale County, Alabama, revealed the presence of spring pygmy sunfish for the first time. At the time the spring was the only known location for the as yet undescribed species, which was referred to as "*Elassoma* species." It was later given the name *Elassoma alabamae*. Four years later a collection was made at a second location, Pryor Spring in Limestone County, Alabama.

In the years that followed the fish was, to all intents and purposes, lost—apparently forever—and it was presumed to be extinct. It was not until 1973 that the species was rediscovered (albeit as a single specimen) in Moss Spring, a tributary of the larger

DATA PANEL

Spring pygmy sunfish

Elassoma alabamae

Family: Elassomatidae

World population: Numbers unknown, but abundant in the very few and restricted localities where it is known to exist

Distribution: Pryor Spring and several other springs and small waterways in Beaverdam Creek, Limestone County, Alabama

Habitat: Densely vegetated clear spring waters

Size: Length: 1.2 in (3 cm)

Form: Male dark brown or blue/black, with 6–8 vertical golden bars on body; female is less colorful. Mature male has a transparent small "window" on posterior section of the dorsal (back) and anal (belly) fins

Diet: Small aquatic invertebrates

Breeding: Territories established by males, whose colors intensify, and attract females.

Intricate courtship display is followed by the spawners aligning themselves side-by-side among fine-leaved vegetation. Eggs are released and fertilized. Most stick to vegetation where they are guarded by the male until they hatch some days later

Related endangered species: Carolina pygmy sunfish (*Elassoma boehlkei*) LRnt; blue-barred pygmy sunfish (*E. okatie*) VU

Status: Not listed by IUCN

Beaverdam Creek in another part of Limestone County. Since then, other locations in the region have yielded further stocks of the spring pygmy sunfish. Despite the newer finds, however, the geographical range of the species remains restricted.

Multiple Threats

The population of spring pygmy sunfish at Cave Spring was discovered during a survey that was carried out by the Tennessee Valley Authority in advance of the construction of a large reservoir, Pickwick Lake. As the lake began to fill up, Cave Spring was gradually flooded, thus wiping out the species from this habitat.

The one other remaining known locality, Pryor Spring, suffered a different, though similarly terminal, fate. An exotic plant species known as Parrot's Feather swamped both the spring and its outflow, leading to widespread flooding of neighboring forests.

Physical removal of the weed proved ineffective. It was followed by chemical treatment, which had more lasting effects, but did not save the spring pygmy sunfish from its last (presumed) refuge in Pryor Spring. Habitat alteration (channeling of the spring), along with pollution as a result of waste dumping, also contributed to the species' disappearance from the area, where it has not been seen since 1941.

All that remained were the more recently discovered populations in Moss Spring and other small springs and tributaries, as well as those in man-made ditches, such as Lowe's Ditch in the Beaverdam Creek system. Even some of these habitats have experienced severe threats, however. In 1976, for example, dredging to create waterholes for cattle led to the destruction of some of the few remaining habitats.

Rescue Plans

As the situation became ever more critical, measures were set in motion to save the species from further decline and possible extinction. In 1984 landowners,

The spring pygmy sunfish has been variously threatened by the construction of a reservoir, the use of chemicals to remove weeds, and dredging to create waterholes for cattle. Its survival has been helped by a successful captive-breeding program.

researchers, and both state and federal scientists were involved in a project that has resulted in the successful reintroduction of the species into one of its former habitats, Pryor Spring. In addition, at least one captive-bred population of the species is being maintained at Conservation Fisheries, Inc., as a backup measure and in an attempt to learn more about the biology of the minuscule egg-layer, which is notoriously difficult to observe in the wild.

The problems in carrying out field observations do not, however, mean that the species is rare in the localities where it exists. Indeed, it is very abundant at these sites; the difficulty arises from both the small size of the fish and the thick aquatic vegetation that obstructs direct studies, as scientists from the Fisheries Section of the Division of Wildlife and Freshwater Fisheries have discovered.

The future for the spring pygmy sunfish looks more hopeful than it did some years ago. Nevertheless, its very restricted distribution in an area that can be dramatically upset by runoff from crop-spraying, fertilizers, siltation, and other habitat-deteriorating factors means that a careful watch must be kept on the remaining wild populations.

Categories of Threat

The status categories that appear in the data panel for each species throughout this book are based on those published by the International Union for the Conservation of Nature (IUCN). They provide a useful guide to the current status of the species in the wild, and governments throughout the world use them when assessing conservation priorities and in policy-making. However, they do not provide automatic legal protection for the species.

Animals are placed in the appropriate category after scientific research. More species are being added all the time, and animals can be moved from one category to another as their circumstances change.

Extinct (EX)

A group of animals is classified as EX when there is no reasonable doubt that the last individual has died.

Extinct in the Wild (EW)

Animals in this category are known to survive only in captivity or as a population established artificially by introduction somewhere well outside its former range. A species is categorized as EW when exhaustive surveys throughout the areas where it used to occur consistently fail to record a single individual. It is important that such searches be carried out over all of the available habitat and during a season or time of day when the animals should be present.

Critically Endangered (CR)

The category CR includes animals facing an extremely high risk of extinction in the wild in the immediate future. It includes any of the following:

• Any species with fewer than 50 individuals, even if the population is stable.
• Any species with fewer than 250 individuals if the population is declining, badly fragmented, or all in one vulnerable group.
• Animals from larger populations that have declined by 80 percent within 10 years (or are predicted to do so) or three generations, whichever is the longer.

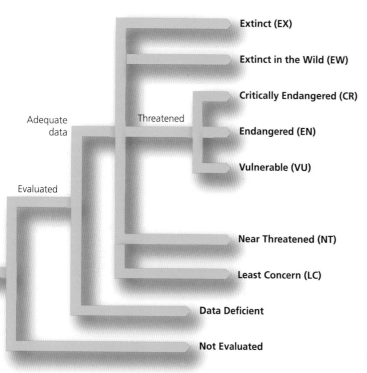

Extinct (EX)

Extinct in the Wild (EW)

Critically Endangered (CR)

Endangered (EN)

Vulnerable (VU)

Near Threatened (NT)

Least Concern (LC)

Data Deficient

Not Evaluated

Adequate data

Threatened

Evaluated

The IUCN categories *of threat. The system displayed has operated for new and reviewed assessments since January 2001.*

• Species living in a very small area—defined as under 39 square miles (100 sq. km).

Endangered (EN)

A species is EN when it is not CR but is nevertheless facing a very high risk of extinction in the wild in the near future. It includes any of the following:

• A species with fewer than 250 individuals remaining, even if the population is stable.

• Any species with fewer than 2,500 individuals if the population is declining, badly fragmented, or all in one vulnerable subpopulation.

• A species whose population is known or expected to decline by 50 percent within 10 years or three generations, whichever is the longer.

• A species whose range is under 1,900 square miles (5,000 sq. km), and whose range, numbers, or population levels are declining, fragmented, or fluctuating wildly.

• Species for which there is a more than 20 percent likelihood of extinction in the next 20 years or five generations, whichever is the longer.

Vulnerable (VU)

A species is VU when it is not CR or EN but is facing a high risk of extinction in the wild in the medium-term future. It includes any of the following:

• A species with fewer than 1,000 mature individuals remaining, even if the population is stable.

• Any species with fewer than 10,000 individuals if the population is declining, badly fragmented, or all in one vulnerable subpopulation.

• A species whose population is known, believed, or expected to decline by 20 percent within 10 years or

Great white sharks *have a fearsome reputation but very few people are killed by them. The species has suffered greatly from hunting and from passive killing. Scientists have struggled to estimate the current population of the great white shark, but believe it to no more than about 10,000.*

three generations, whichever is the longer.
• A species whose range is less than 772 square miles (20,000 sq. km), and whose range, numbers, or population structure are declining, fragmented, or fluctuating wildly.
• Species for which there is a more than 10 percent likelihood of extinction in the next 100 years.

Near Threatened/Least Concern (since 2001)

In January 2001 the classification of lower-risk species was changed. Near Threatened (NT) and Least Concern (LC) were introduced as separate categories. They replaced the previous Lower Risk (LR) category with its subdivisions of Conservation Dependent (LRcd), Near Threatened (LRnt), and Least Concern (LRlc). From January 2001 all new assessments and reassessments must adopt NT or LC if relevant. But the older categories still apply to many animals until they are reassessed, and will also be found in this book.
• Near Threatened (NT)
Animals that do not qualify for CR, EN, or VU categories now but are close to qualifying or are likely to qualify for a threatened category in the future.
• Least Concern (LC)
Animals that have been evaluated and do not qualify for CR, EN, VU, or NT categories.

Lower Risk (before 2001)

• Conservation Dependent (LRcd)
Animals whose survival depends on an existing conservation program
• Near Threatened (LRnt)
Animals for which there is no conservation program but that are close to qualifying for VU category.

By monitoring *populations of threatened animals like this American rosy boa, biologists help keep the IUCN Red List up to date.*

Overfishing *and the destruction of the fishes' habitats have seriously reduced the numbers of several species of sturgeon.*

• Least Concern (LRlc)
Species that are not conservation dependent or near threatened.

Data Deficient (DD)

A species or population is DD when there is not enough information on abundance and distribution to assess the risk of extinction. In some cases, when the species is thought to live only in a small area, or a considerable period of time has passed since the species was last recorded, it may be placed in a threatened category as a precaution.

Not Evaluated (NE)

Such animals have not yet been assessed.

Note: a colored panel in each entry in this book indicates the current level of threat to the species. The two new categories (NT and LC) and two of the earlier Lower Risk categories (LRcd and LRnt) are included within the band LR; the old LRlc is included along with Data Deficient (DD) and Not Evaluated (NE) under "Other," abbreviated to "O."

CITES *lists animals in the major groups in three Appendices, depending on the level of threat posed by international trade.*

	Appendix I	Appendix II	Appendix III
Mammals	277 species 16 subspecies 14 populations	295 species 12 subspecies 12 populations	45 species 8 subspecies
Birds	152 species 11 subspecies 2 populations	1,268 species 6 subspecies 1 populations	35 species
Reptiles	75 species 5 subspecies 6 populations	527 species 4 subspecies 4 populations	55 species
Amphibians	16 species	98 species	
Fish	15 species	71 species	
Invertebrates	62 species 4 subspecies	2,100 species 1 subspecies	17 species

CITES APPENDICES

Appendix I lists the most endangered of traded species, namely those that are threatened with extinction and will be harmed by continued trade. These species are usually protected in their native countries and can only be imported or exported with a special permit. Permits are required to cover the whole transaction—both exporter and importer must prove that there is a compelling scientific justification for moving the animal from one country to another. This includes transferring animals between zoos for breeding purposes. Permits are only issued when it can be proved that the animal was legally acquired and that the remaining population will not be harmed by the loss.

Appendix II includes species that are not currently threatened with extinction, but that could easily become so if trade is not carefully controlled. Some common animals are listed here if they resemble endangered species so closely that criminals could try to sell the rare species pretending they were a similar common one. Permits are required to export such animals, with requirements similar to those Appendix I species.

Appendix III species are those that are at risk or protected in at least one country. Other nations may be allowed to trade in animals or products, but they may need to prove that they come from safe populations.

CITES designations are not always the same for every country. In some cases individual countries can apply for special permission to trade in a listed species. For example, they might have a safe population of an animal that is very rare elsewhere. Some African countries periodically apply for permission to export large quantities of elephant tusks that have been in storage for years, or that are the product of a legal cull of elephants. This is controversial because it creates an opportunity for criminals to dispose of black market ivory by passing it off as coming from one of those countries where elephant products are allowed to be exported. If you look up the African elephant, you will see that it is listed as CITES I, II, and III, depending on the country location of the different populations.

Organizations

The human race is undoubtedly nature's worst enemy, but we can also help limit the damage caused by the rapid increase in our numbers and activities. There have always been people eager to protect the world's beautiful places and to preserve its most special animals, but it is only quite recently that the conservation message has begun to have a real effect on everyday life, government policy, industry, and agriculture.

Early conservationists were concerned with preserving nature for the benefit of people. They acted with an instinctive sense of what was good for nature and people, arguing for the preservation of wilderness and animals in the same way as others argued for the conservation of historic buildings or gardens. The study of ecology and environmental science did not really take off until the mid-20th century, and it took a long time for the true scale of our effect in the natural world to become apparent. Today the conservation of wildlife is based on far greater scientific understanding, but the situation has become much more complex and urgent in the face of human development.

By the mid-20th century extinction was becoming an immediate threat. Animals such as the passenger pigeon, quagga, and thylacine had disappeared despite last-minute attempts to save them. More and more species were discovered to be at risk, and species-focused conservation groups began to appear. In the early days there was little that any of these organizations could do but campaign against direct killing. Later they became a kind of conservation emergency service—rushing to the aid of seriously threatened animals in an attempt to save the species. But as time went on, broader environmental issues began to receive the urgent attention they needed. Research showed time and time again that saving species almost always comes down to addressing the

Conservation *organizations range from government departments in charge of national parks, such as Yellowstone National Park (right), the oldest in the United States, to local initiatives set up to protect endangered birds. Here (above) a man in Peru climbs a tree to check on the nest of a harpy eagle discovered near his village.*

problem of habitat loss. The world is short of space, and ensuring that there is enough for all the species is very difficult.

Conservation is not just about animals and plants, nor even the protection of whole ecological systems. Conservation issues are so broad that they touch almost every aspect of our lives, and successful measures often depend on the expertise of biologists, ecologists, economists, diplomats, lawyers, social scientists, and businesspeople. Conservation is all about cooperation and teamwork. Often it is also about helping people benefit from taking care of their wildlife. The organizations involved vary from small groups of a few dozen enthusiasts in local communities to vast, multinational operations.

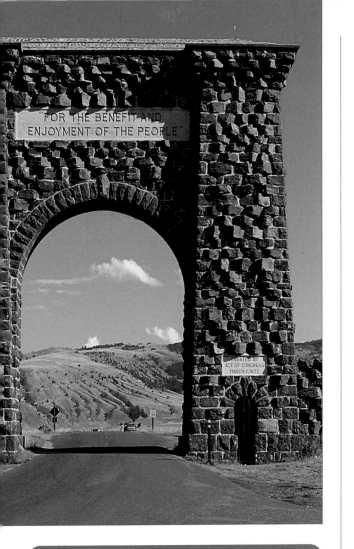

THE IUCN

With so much activity based in different countries, it is important to have a worldwide overview, some way of coordinating what goes on in different parts of the planet. That is the role of the International Union for the Conservation of Nature (IUCN), also referred to as the World Conservation Union. It began life as the International Union for the Preservation of Nature in 1948, becoming the IUCN in 1956. It is relatively new compared to the Sierra Club, Flora & Fauna International, and the Royal Society for the Protection of Birds. It was remarkable in that its founder members included governments, government agencies, and nongovernmental organizations. In the

years following the appalling destruction of World War II, the IUCN was born out of a desire to draw a line under the horrors of the past and to act together to safeguard the future.

The mission of the IUCN is to influence, encourage, and assist societies throughout the world to conserve the diversity of nature and natural systems. It seeks to ensure that the use of natural resources is fair and ecologically sustainable. Based in Switzerland, the IUCN has over 1,000 permanent staff and the help of 11,000 volunteer experts from about 180 countries. The work of the IUCN is split into six commissions, which deal with protected areas, policy-making, ecosystem management, education, environmental law, and species survival. The Species Survival Commission (SSC) has almost 7,000 members, all experts in the study of plants and animals. Within the SSC there are Specialist Groups concerned with the conservation of different types of animals, from cats to flamingos, deer, ducks, bats, and crocodiles. Some particularly well-studied animals, such as the African elephant and the polar bear, have their own specialist groups.

Perhaps the best-known role of the IUCN SSC is in the production of the Red Data Books, or Red Lists. First published in 1966, the books were designed to be easily updated, with details of each species on a different page that could be removed and replaced as new information came to light.

By 2010 the Red Lists include information on about 45,000 types of animal, of which almost 10,000 are threatened with extinction. Gathering this amount of information together is a

The IUCN Red Lists *of threatened species are published online and can be accessed at:* *http://www. iucnredlist.org*

huge task, but it provides an invaluable conservation resource. The Red Lists are continually updated and are now available on the World Wide Web. The Red Lists are the basis for the categories of threat used in this book.

CITES

CITES is the Convention on International Trade in Endangered Species of Wild Fauna and Flora (also known as the Washington Convention, since it first came into force after an international meeting in Washington D.C. in 1973). Currently 175 nations have agreed to implement the CITES regulations. Exceptions to the convention include Iraq and North Korea, which, for the time being at least, have few trading links with the rest of the world. Trading in animals and their body parts has been a major factor in the decline of some of the world's rarest species. The IUCN categories draw attention to the status of rare species, but they do not confer any legal protection. That is done through national laws.

Conventions serve as international laws. In the case of CITES, lists (called Appendices) are agreed on internationally and reviewed every few years. The Appendices list the species that are threatened by international trade. Animals are assigned to Appendix I when all trade is forbidden. Any specimens of these species, alive or dead (or skins, feathers, etc.), will be confiscated by customs at international borders, seaports, or airports. Appendix II species can be traded internationally, but only under strict controls. Wildlife trade is often valuable in the rural economy, and this raises difficult questions about the relative importance of animals and people. Nevertheless, traders who ignore CITES rules risk heavy fines or imprisonment. Some rare species—even those with the highest IUCN categories (many bats and frogs, for example)—may have no CITES protection simply because they have no commercial value. Trade is then not really a threat.

The Greenpeace ship, *seen here in Antarctica, travels to areas of conservation concern and helps draw worldwide media attention to environmental issues.*

WILDLIFE CONSERVATION ORGANIZATIONS

BirdLife International
BirdLife International is a partnership of 60 organizations working in more than 100 countries. Most partners are national nongovernmental conservation groups such as the Canadian Nature Federation. Others include large bird charities such as the Royal Society for the Protection of Birds in Britain. By working together within BirdLife International, even small organizations can be effective globally as well as on a local scale. BirdLife International is a member of the IUCN.
Web site: http://www.birdlife.org

Conservation International (CI)
Founded in 1987, Conservation International works closely with the IUCN and has a similar multinational approach. CI offers help in the world's most threatened biodiversity hot spots.
Web site: http://conservation.org

Durrell Wildlife Conservation Trust (DWCT)
Another IUCN member, the Durrell Wildlife Conservation Trust was founded by the British naturalist and author Gerald Durrell in 1963. The trust is based at Durrell's world-famous zoo on Jersey in the Channel Islands. Jersey was the world's first zoo dedicated solely to the conservation of endangered species. Breeding programs at the zoo have helped stabilize populations of some of the world's most endangered animals. The trust trains conservationists from many countries and works to secure areas of natural habitat to which animals can be returned. Jersey Zoo and the DWCT were instrumental in saving numerous species from extinction, including the pink pigeon, Mauritius kestrel, Waldrapp ibis, St. Lucia parrot, and the Telfair's skink and other reptiles.
Web site: http://durrell.org

Fauna & Flora International (FFI)
Founded in 1903, this organization has had various name changes. It began life as a society for protecting large mammals, but has broadened its scope. It was involved in saving the Arabian oryx from extinction.
Web site: http://www.fauna-flora.org

National Audubon Society
John James Audubon was an American naturalist and wildlife artist who died in 1851, 35 years before the society that bears his name was founded. The first Audubon Society was established by George Bird Grinnell in protest against the appalling overkill of birds for meat, feathers, and sport. By the end of the 19th century there were Audubon Societies in 15 states, and they later became part of the National Audubon Society, which funds scientific research programs, publishes

WILDLIFE CONSERVATION ORGANIZATIONS

magazines and journals, manages wildlife sanctuaries, and advises state and federal governments on conservation issues.
Web site: http://www.audubon.org

Pressure Groups

Friends of the Earth, founded in Britain in 1969, and Greenpeace, founded in 1971 in British Columbia, were the first environmental pressure groups to become internationally recognized. Greenpeace became known for "direct, nonviolent actions," which drew attention to major conservation issues. (For example, campaigners steered boats between the harpoon guns of whalers and their prey.)

The organizations offer advice to governments and corporations, and help those that seek to protect the environment, while continuing to name, shame, and campaign against those who do not.

Royal Society for the Protection of Birds

This organization was founded in the 1890s to campaign against the slaughter of birds to supply feathers for the fashion trade. It now has a wider role and has become Britain's premier wildlife conservation organization, with over a million members. It is involved in international activities, particularly in the protection of birds that migrate to Britain.
Web site: http://www.rspb.org.uk

The Sierra Club

The Sierra Club was started in 1892 by John Muir and is still going strong. Muir, a Scotsman by birth, is often thought of as the founder of the conservation movement, especially in the United States, where he campaigned for the preservation of wilderness. It was through his efforts that the first national parks, including Yosemite,

Sequoia, and Mount Rainier, were established. Today the Sierra Club remains dedicated to the preservation of wild places for the benefit of wildlife and the enjoyment of people.
Web site: http://www.sierraclub.org

World Wide Fund for Nature (WWF)

The World Wide Fund for Nature, formerly the World Wildlife Fund, was born in 1961. It was a joint venture between the IUCN, several existing conservation organizations, and a number of successful businesspeople. Unlike many charities, WWF was big, well-funded, and high profile from the beginning. Its familiar giant panda emblem ranks alongside those of the Red Cross, Mercedes Benz, or Coca-Cola in terms of instant international recognition.
Web site: http://www.wwf.org

GLOSSARY

adaptation Features of an animal that adjust it to its environment; may be produced by evolution—e.g., camouflage coloration

adaptive radiation Where a group of closely related animals (e.g., members of a family) have evolved differences from each other so that they can survive in different niches

adult A fully grown sexually mature animal

ambient Describing the conditions around an animal, e.g., the water temperature for a fish or the air temperature for a land animal

anadromous Fish that spend most of their life at sea but migrate into fresh water for breeding, e.g., salmon

anterior The front part of an animal

biodiversity The variety of species and the variation within them

biome A major world landscape characterized by having similar plants and animals living in it, e.g., desert, rain forest, forest

catadromous Fish that spend most of their life in fresh water but migrate to the sea for spawning, e.g., eels

caudal fin The tail fin in fish

class A large taxonomic group of related animals. Mammals, insects, and reptiles are all classes of animals

cloaca Cavity in the pelvic region into which the alimentary canal, genital, and urinary ducts open

dispersal The scattering of young animals going to live away from where they were born and brought up

DNA (deoxyribonucleic acid) The substance that makes up the main part of the chromosomes of all living things; contains the genetic code that is handed down from generation to generation

dorsal Relating to the back or spinal part of the body; usually the upper surface

ecosystem A whole system in which plants, animals, and their environment interact

ectotherm Animal that relies on external heat sources to raise body temperature; also known as "cold-blooded"

endemic Found only in one geographical area, nowhere else

eutrophication An increase in the nutrient chemicals (nitrate, phosphate, etc.) in water, sometimes occurring naturally and sometimes caused by human activities, e.g., by the release of sewage or agricultural fertilizers

extinction Process of dying out at the end of which the very last individual dies, and the species is lost forever

family A group of closely related species that often also look quite similar. Zoological family names always end in -idae. Also used to describe a social group within a species comprising parents and their offspring

gene The basic unit of heredity, enabling one generation to pass on characteristics to its offspring

genus (genera, pl.) A group of closely related species

gill Respiratory organ that absorbs oxygen from the water. External gills occur in tadpoles. Internal gills occur in most fish

hybrid Offspring of two closely related species that can breed; it is sterile and so cannot produce offspring

ichthyologist Zoologist specializing in the study of fish

indigenous Living naturally in a region; native (i.e., not an introduced species)

invertebrates Animals that have no backbone (or other bones) inside their body, e.g., mollusks, insects, jellyfish, crabs

juvenile A young animal that has not yet reached breeding age

krill Planktonic shrimps

labyrinth Specialized auxiliary (extra) breathing organ found in some fish

lateral line system A system of pores running along a fish's body. These pores lead to nerve endings that allow a fish to sense vibrations in the water and help it locate prey, detect predators, avoid obstacles, and so on. Also found in amphibians

livebearer Animal that gives birth to fully developed young (usually refers to reptiles or fish)

marine Living in the sea

metabolic rate Rate the rate at which chemical activities occur within animals, including the exchange of gasses in respiration and the liberation of energy from food

operculum A cover consisting of bony plates that covers the gills of fish

order A subdivision of a class of animals, consisting of a series of animal families

organism Any member of the animal or plant kingdom; a body that has life

oviparous Producing eggs that hatch outside the body of the mother (in fish, reptiles, birds, and monotremes)

parasite An animal or plant that lives on or within the body of another (the host) from which it obtains nourishment. The host is often harmed by the association

pelagic Living in the upper waters of the open sea or large lakes

phylum Zoological term for a major grouping of animal classes. The whole animal kingdom is divided into about 30 phyla, of which the vertebrates form part of just one

plankton Animals and plants drifting in open water; many are minute

population A distinct group of animals of the same species or all the animals of that species

posterior The hind end or behind another structure

spawning The laying and fertilizing of eggs by fish and amphibians and some mollusks

speciation The origin of species; the diverging of two similar organisms through reproduction down through the generations into different forms resulting in a new species

species A group of animals that look similar and can breed with each other to produce fertile offspring

subspecies A subpopulation of a single species whose members are similar to each other but differ from the typical form for that species; often called a race

substrate A medium to which fixed animals are attached under water, such as rocks onto which barnacles and mussels are attached, or plants are anchored in, e.g., gravel, mud, or sand in which aquatic plants have their roots embedded

swim bladder A gas or air-filled bladder in fish; by taking in or exhaling air, the fish can alter its buoyancy

symbiosis A close relationship between members of two species from which both partners benefit

ventral Of or relating to the front part or belly of an animal (see dorsal)

vertebrate Animal with a backbone (e.g., fish, mammal, reptile), usually with skeleton made of bones, but sometimes softer cartilage

FURTHER RESEARCH

Books

Fish
Buttfield, Helen, *The Secret Lives of Fishes*, Abrams, U.S., 2000

Dawes, John, and Campbell, Andrew, eds., *The New Encyclopedia of Aquatic Life, Facts On File*, New York, U.S., 2004

Greenberg, Paul, *Four Fish: The Future of the Last Wild Food,* Penguin Press, New York, U.S., 2010

Montgomery, David R., *King of Fish: The Thousand-Year Run of Salmon*, Westview Press, Boulder, U.S., 2003

Mammals
Macdonald, David, *The New Encyclopedia of Mammals,* Oxford University Press, Oxford, U.K., 2009

Payne, Roger, *Among Whales*, Bantam Press, U.S., 1996

Reeves, R. R., and Leatherwood, S., *The Sierra Club Handbook of Whales and Dolphins of the World*, Sierra Club, U.S., 1983

Sherrow, Victoria, and Cohen, Sandee, *Endangered Mammals of North America*, Twenty-First Century Books, U.S., 1995

Whitaker, J. O., Audubon Society
Field Guide to North American Mammals, Alfred A. Knopf, New York, U.S., 1996

Wilson, Don E., Mittermeier, Russell A., *Handbook of Mammals of the World Vol 1,* Lynx Edicions, Barcelona, Spain, 2009

Birds
Attenborough, David, *The Life of Birds,* BBC Books, London, U.K., 1998

BirdLife International, *Threatened Birds of the World*, Lynx Edicions, Barcelona, Spain and BirdLife International, Cambridge, U.K., 2000

del Hoyo, J., Elliott, A., and Sargatal, J., eds., *Handbook of Birds of the World Vols 1 to 15,* Lynx Edicions, Barcelona, Spain, 1992–2010

Dunn, Jon, and Alderfer, Jonathan K., *National Geographic Field Guide to the Birds of North America,* National Geographic Society, Washington D.C., United States, 2006.

Stattersfield, A., Crosby, M., Long, A., and Wege, D., eds., *Endemic Bird Areas of the World: Priorities for Biodiversity Conservation*, BirdLife International, Cambridge, U.K., 1998

Reptiles and Amphibians
Corbett, Keith, *Conservation of European Reptiles and Amphibians*, Christopher Helm, London, U.K., 1989

Corton, Misty, *Leopard and Other South African Tortoises*, Carapace Press, London, U.K., 2000

Hofrichter, Robert, *Amphibians: The World of Frogs, Toads, Salamanders, and Newts*, Firefly Books, Canada, 2000

Murphy, J. B., Adler, K., and Collins, J. T. (eds.), *Captive Management and Conservation of Reptiles and Amphibians*, Society for the Study of Amphibians and Reptiles, Ithaca, New York, 1994

Stafford, Peter, *Snakes*, Natural History Museum, London, U.K., 2000

Insects
Eaton, Eric R. and Kaufman, Kenn. *Kaufman Field Guide to Insects of North America*, Houghton Mifflin, New York, U.S., 2007

Pyle, Robert Michael, National Audubon Society *Field Guide to North American Butterflies*, Pyle, Robert Michael, A. Knopf, New York, U.S., 1995

General
Allaby, Michael, *A Dictionary of Ecology*, Oxford University Press, New York, U.S., 2010

Douglas, Dougal, and others, *Atlas of Life on Earth*, Barnes & Noble, New York, U.S., 2001

Web sites
http://www.nature.nps.gov/ U.S. National Park Service wildlife site

http://www.ummz.lsa.umich-edu/
umich.edu/ University of Michigan Museum of Zoology animal diversity web. Search for pictures and information about animals by class, family, and common name

http://www.cites.org/ CITES and IUCN listings. Search for animals by order, family, genus, species, or common name. Location by country and explanation of reasons for listings

http://www.cmc-ocean.org Facts, figures, and quizzes about marine life

www.darwinfoundation.org/ Charles Darwin Research Center

http://www.fws.gov.endangered Information about endangered animals and plants from the U.S. Fish and Wildlife Service, the organization in charge of 94 million acres of wildlife refuges

http://www.endangeredspecie.com
Information, links, books, and publications about rare and endangered species. Also includes information about conservation efforts and organizations

http://www.ewt.org.za Endangered South African wildlife

http://www.iucn.org Details of species, IUCN listings, and IUCN publications. Link to online Red Lists of threatened species at: www.iucnredlist.org

http://www.pbs.org/journeytoamazonia The Amazonian rain forest and its unrivaled biodiversity

http://wildfishconservancy.org News of wild salmon and other fish species in the Pacific Northwest

INDEX

Words and page numbers in **bold type** indicate main references to the various topics.